UNDER
the
GOLDEN COD

Atop the Old North Church in Marblehead,

A weathervane, the image of the cod,

Swings seaward in the frequent salty airs,

Man's humble never-failing friend the cod,

Which shows the compass of the love of God.

---

from "All Homage to the Cod" by Earl F. Cook

The codfish weathervane atop the Old North Church in Marblehead was originally installed on the Second Meeting House erected in 1695. It was moved to its present location in 1824. Designed and constructed by an unknown artisan, the full-formed copper body of the cod is 52 inches long and is gilded.

UNDER the GOLDEN COD

A shared history of the Old North Church and the town of Marblehead, Massachusetts

1635–1985

Researched and written for

The 350th Anniversary
Book Committee

PHOENIX PUBLISHING

Canaan, New Hampshire

Under the Golden Cod.

Includes index.
1. Old North Church (Marblehead Mass.) — History. 2. Marblehead (Mass.) — History. I. 350th Anniversary Book Committee.
BX7255.M2956U53   1984   285.8'7445   84-7821
ISBN 0-914659-05-7

Printed in the United States of America
by Courier Printing Company
Binding by New Hampshire Bindery
Design by A. L. Morris

CONTENTS

ACKNOWLEDGMENTS

It was with considerable concern in June 1983 that I accepted the chairmanship of a committee to produce a book commemorating 350 years of service by the Old North Church. Thanks to the excellent committee and the enthusiastic response from the many who contributed to the undertaking, an unusual historical volume has been written and is in the process of publication.

I am particularly indebted to the members of this Book Committee for their time, talents, contributions, and advice; specifically to Randy Niehoff for his valuable suggestions and encouragement; to Dorothy Learoyd, our treasurer and promotion chairman; to Bob Gotschall, general chairman of the 350th Anniversary Committee for his unstinting support; and to my wife Ruth, our secretary, who spent untold hours recording minutes and typing both minutes and manuscript.

I would also like to express my thanks to Bowden Osborne who generously provided so many pictures from his historic collection, to Marie Hughes for her assistance in typing the manuscript, and to the many others too numerous to mention who helped in countless ways.

Finally we express our collective gratitude to the authors for their many hours of conscientious research, writing, and hard work, without which there would have been no publication. They included: Reverend Eugene R. Arnould, Deborah R. Caulkins, R. Brooks Corl, Donald A. Doliber, John H. Ferguson, Robert E. Gotschall, Reverend C. Francis Hood, Ralph L. Keller, Dorothy B. Learoyd, Priscilla Sawyer Lord, Reverend Randall H. Niehoff, Charlotte Ferguson Roads, Irma and George Sprague, Jerri Strozier, and Joan Thompson.

John H. Ferguson
Chairman

Marblehead, Massachusetts
January 11, 1984

vi

FOREWORD

DESCARTES OBSERVED that every great book is the product of a single mind. On the contrary, Yankee wisdom asserts that great churches and towns are the product of many minds. This book is about something far greater than could be envisioned from a solitary point of view. It is a kind of New England seacoast journal about a living community whose many personal stories have been woven together by their shared experience in 350 years of continuous history.

Like a marvelous tapestry three and one-half centuries in the making, the threads of individual lives have mingled to create a seamless bond. Stepping back to try to glimpse a vision of the whole, the life of this congregation displays the reassurance of faith, the colors of independence, and the warmth of tolerance. These three themes — faith, independence, and tolerance — mark the threads used to "spin the yarn" of the story of the First Church of Christ in Marblehead; and these are the ties that bind together the history of Old North Church and grand old Marblehead.

All this life, and more than could ever be recorded properly, has occurred under the symbol of the Golden Cod. The actual fifty-two inch long codfish weathervane has swung in the wind above the church meeting house and its old town since 1695. But, figuratively, the humble smiling fish has served as a dual symbol for the town and the church since each was gathered. The plentiful codfish was the economic mainstay of colonial New England; and the precious fish has been a symbol of Christianity since the first century. From the Cod's lofty perspective this unique Marblehead history has unfolded below. Our book has been written to draw attention to this long story. As we focus on the themes revealed herein it is our hope that we have created a record that would make our forebears proud and our posterity inspired.

Dr. Randall H. Niehoff

Senior Minister

Marblehead, Massachusetts
January 15, 1984

UNDER
the
GOLDEN COD

TO THE

Flock in MARBLEHEAD,

Over which the Holy Ghost hath made
me an Overseer.

Dearly Beloved in our Lord Jesus Christ,

Here present you with those Discourses, which so many of you have desired to be made publick: they were firstly calculated for you; and if they may in any measure assist you, and yours, in your spiritual Warfare, that you may run well and obtain the Crown, I shall not be uneasy at venturing them abroad, in an Age wherein almost every one sets himself up for a Critick.

The Subjects are weighty, and of universal Concernment. I have not placed them in the Order, in which they were first delivered to you; but so as they may best carry some Relation or Connexion.

In the First, you have the Truth of the Christian Religion, the best of Religions, confirmed; so far as a single Sermon would allow me to go

A 2

Foreword from Parson John Barnard's book of sermon discourses published in 1727.

I

English Roots

S OME PEOPLE in the seventeenth century were not happy with the Church of England. There were those who did not care much about church at all, and there were some who cared so much that they wanted to change it or leave it.

In the Elizabethan Renaissance, many people's ultimate concern shifted from God's kingdom on earth to a person's place on earth. These people did not disturb the crown; rather, they were congruent with the political scene. The court was a place of worldly enjoyment. Music, dancing, plays, games and cards, feasts and ceremonies revolved around the monarch. There was little time for church.

Others were unhappy about the church for different reasons. They did not feel that King Henry VIII's reform had gone far enough. He had broken the papal tie and replaced it with himself. Elizabeth and James I inherited the authority which made them heads of the church as well as of the state, and they intended to maintain it. The reformers wanted to simplify the church according to the gospel, "Without the mixture of men's invention," Bradford said. They wanted to rid the church of priests, bishops, canon, and ceremonies. Their dissent was a threat to the crown and was viewed as heresy, ultimately a capital offense.

Supporters of more church reform were known as Puritans, a sect of Protestants. They advocated reform within the church. Others saw little hope for reform and wanted to separate from the Church of England.

It is February 1607 and a young woman walks across the fields of Cornwall. A mist has rolled in off the sea and has crept quietly up into the hills. Gorse and bracken cover the fields. There are not many trees, just a few weather-torn, stunted old trunks folding away from the channel's winds. Her cloak is open, but she hardly needs it. The day is damp but not cold. Rhododendron and gorse are in flower and seem even brighter on the gray day. There is no winter to fear in Cornwall, only the storms.

Some would take pains to skirt around one part of the path she is on, but she is braver than most and in a hurry. Yet her heart beats faster as she approaches the strange stones that loom up in the mist. Most lean fingerlike, as tall as she and covered with lichen. Another is round with a perfect hole all the way through the center. A sense of magic always lurks in this place, whether good or evil she cannot tell.

Sand stings her face as she nears the dunes, and she turns her head lest she get sand in her eyes. Reaching the crest of a dune, she crouches down in the tufted grass and looks out over the sea. The wind has changed and the mist slips apart, exposing the long dark coast which twines in and out beside the water. A gull dives. It is the only movement.

She watches and waits, her eyes fixed on what would be the horizon but can be seen only during the intervals when the mist breaks. Boats bob in the harbor below and to her right, but she is blind to them. Finally she sighs and gets up to leave. The mist becomes a sail as a small boat makes its way inland. She is off, sliding down sand dunes and across a field. She heads for the harbor, plucking daffodils as she runs. The boat is just pulling up to dock when she arrives, panting. The familiar face appears behind nets, and a smile as wide as the sky spreads on it like sunshine. The dark-haired, sturdy lad swings up the boat's side and over, then becomes shy from being so dirty. She offers him daffodils. He sniffs and gives them back, jumps into the boat, and unloads the catch so quickly the others laugh at him.

When the work is through they walk up the hill together, and he tells her about the storm that came from nowhere and how they sought refuge on an island. In the tavern they met other fishermen who talked about the New World, how they went in the spring and returned late in the summer with a catch so great people thought they were bewitched.

"But they were not," he assures her. "It is a wonderful, warm place, bright with sunshine and more trees than anyone would imagine were possible. It is also a lonely, wild country. The only people are natives who were supposed to be friendly. The good fishing, a chance to travel and see new sights . . ."

He finds himself unable to explain more, especially with her head down and she being so silent. He assures her that he will be back in the fall, for no one could survive the winters. Right now they would be waist deep in snow. He pleads, he promises, but she does not speak, and then he too is silent.

Slowly they walk until they reach the western point and can go no farther. Once again she surveys the mist that hides the water between Cornwall and the New World. The soft gray mist which surrounds them parts, and a slate sea now surrounds them on three sides. The corners of her mouth turn up, and she looks at him, her face alight.

"As soon as the first settlers go to live there, I will go too. It will be our home."

His grin returns, and he strews the daffodils over the cliff and into the waves below.

Most of the original settlers of Marblehead were from Cornwall, Devon, Guernsey, and Jersey, the southern coastal region of England; a few were from Lincolnshire. They were fishermen and had fished the New England coast for years before Plymouth was established. They did not settle, however, until after Salem became a town. Rather, the fishermen set up camps in the late spring and left before fall winds would make returning difficult.

Fishing had always been a livelihood in Cornwall. Fish were caught the same way in the seventeenth century as they are today. The women salted them down for winter storage and for shipping abroad. Women's part in the process must have been greatly missed in the fishing camps.

Cornwall's climate is quite different from New England's. It is not uncommon for daffodils and rhododendron to bloom in the mild, misty winter. The summers in Cornwall are cool and misty, too, very different from New England's warm, sunny days.

The two landscapes are similar. Rocky cliffs and jagged shorelines, sandy beaches, and sand dunes compare with the North Shore and the Cape. The remarkable difference in 1607 would have been the lack of trees on England's coast. Timber, greatly valued for building and firewood, would have been shipped long since. It was too accessible by the water.

Mysterious stones described on the walk are found scattered all over Cornwall, and their meaning is open to conjecture. Perhaps they are early tombs from some forgotten religion. Their presence has left an impact on all Cornish and has visibly preserved the ancient lore and intuitive perception of past things.

The Cornish are very religious but perhaps not in the traditional sense.

They are an aloof, independent people on their peninsula, and they accepted Christianity as easily as they had embraced the Celtic cult. They wove both together, along with their Mediterranean beliefs, and found familiarity in the mystique of the mass. When the Reformation took away the signs, symbols, and rituals, the Cornish turned back to an older religion. Suddenly spirits stirred on hilltops and in the earth's hollows. Magic was practiced as never before. For example, the Cornish had special cures which they used until only recent times. For smallpox or measles, a live fowl would be hung in the patient's bedroom with its feathers plucked. Within twenty-four hours the rash would transfer to the still living bird, and it would then turn black and die while the patient recovered.

Charmers healed and witches cursed during the seventeenth century. Misfortune was often the fault of a witch, and many Cornish villages employed conjurers to secretly discover the witch's identity. Owls were birds of ill omen. The hare contained either the spirit of a dead woman or was a witch in disguise. If a rabbit or hare were even mentioned to a fisherman who was out at sea, he considered his luck destroyed, pulled in his nets, and went home.

Superstition aside, the Cornish did not fit into conventional religion, neither Anglican nor Puritan. They continued life on their own terms in Marblehead as they had done in England. They would have been closer to the Plymouth Separatists. This may have nettled the Salem ministers, but the fishermen's value was too important for Salem to interfere. Fish was money in Salem's pocket.

The Cornish woman who made the pact with her sweetheart to come with the first settlers would probably have been middle-aged when she arrived with their nearly grown children. Marble Harbor was settled in 1629. Salem was the closest settlement, and though it was only a village, Salem included Marble Harbor in its township. Although the wilderness was being pushed back along the New England coast, the first settlers in the fishing community probably did little socializing outside their own. They retained their natural Cornish and Channel Islands reserve. Marble Harbor changed its name to Marblehead and had some of the same geographical qualities the settlers had grown up with in England. Like the Cornish peninsula, it was surrounded by water from its own harbor and that of another town (in this case, Salem). Like the island people's home, it had its "Necke" which supplied the fishing vessels with water from a spring. It is not surprising that the settlers kept their odd accents and customs. Their independent spirits found a geographical home on the coast of New England.

The first settlers in Marblehead considered themselves English and became Americans only as the slow process of adaptation took place. They built their homes in the style of their ancestors, being grateful for the abundant supply of wood. Wood, a better insulator than stone, was used for heating as well. Fire was such an important part of their life that they appreciated the New World's natural wealth in its forests.

If the houses were small, that would not have been unusual. Many homes in England had only one room. Compared to today a different attitude existed toward privacy in the seventeenth century, and activities were not separated by rooms.

It is easy to suppose that the settlers missed ready access to supplies and goods. However, back home in Cornwall they purchased in a different fashion than we do today. Needs developed for months until clearly formulated, and then a year's supply of goods was purchased. Waiting for the ship was similar to their former style of shopping.

If the first settlers did not bring much with them, they did not leave many material goods at home either. Most household goods could be fitted into a single chest, and replacing the rest would be easy. Furniture was not elaborate, and one of the most important articles would be a cast-iron pot which hung over the fire. Seventeenth-century meals were mainly stews and soups; bread was baked in outdoor kilns; beer was drunk like water and could be brewed from almost any grain or roots at hand.

Many of the first settlers' basic needs were met in Marblehead: clean water, abundant wood and fish, plenty of space for all, and complete freedom. However, those pioneer fishermen left behind parents, friends, and sometimes children and spouses. Being homesick is as painful as any illness and as real; it is an indefinable longing for everything that is home.

Home was created by the arrival of families—women and children, whose presence was not underestimated. The arrival of families turned a fishing camp into a settlement; the difference may have been visible only in a bowl of wild flowers sitting on a table. They were a courageous people, those first settlers who chose to establish a community in an unfamiliar land and who gave Marblehead its style.

The establishment of families within the infant town emphasized the need for a church nearby. Not only was considerable time required to walk to Naugus Head and either row or sail across to Salem, but the winds and the cold of winter presented real threats to health and even to life.

It is small wonder, then, that only six years after the first settlers arrived the need to found a church in Marblehead moved the inhabitants to look about for a minister. The name of the Reverend John Avery of Newbury had come to the attention of the people, and he was invited to become the town's first pastor. He declined the first call, but when it was repeated he accepted, and in August 1635, together with his family of eight, set sail for Marblehead as passengers on a Marblehead fishing vessel owned by Isaac Allerton. Unfortunately, the vessel was overtaken by winds and waves of hurricane force and was wrecked off Cape Ann on what is known as Avery Ledge and is today marked by a bellbuoy. The entire Avery family died in the disaster.

This calamity was a profound shock to those who had gathered together the nucleus of the First Church. The exact time required to obtain a religious teacher is not known, but the records do show that in somewhat less than four years religious services were being conducted in Marblehead.

2

The Puritan Heritage

THE PURITAN MOVEMENT started in sixteenth-century England as a political movement within the Anglican church. The Puritans were a "reform" group who advocated freedom of religious expression for both clergy and lay members. Calvinism gradually influenced their theology, with predestination and an absolute moral code being the principal contributions. Within the movement there were some who advocated separation from the Anglicans to form a new sect, but this group apparently was a minority in England at the time of Marblehead's settlement.

Persecution by King James I, a weak and cowardly man who imagined the Puritans a threat to his power, drove many early Puritan ministers to establish congregations "in exile," first in Holland, and finally in the colonies of New England. The ascension of James's son, King Charles I, led to more intense quarrels between the king and the Puritans and, ultimately, to civil war in England. Both William Walton, Marblehead's first minister, and Hugh Peters, minister at the church in Salem at the time Walton arrived, were profoundly affected by these political troubles in England.

The English Civil War pitted King Charles I and his established Church of England against the Puritans, led by Oliver Cromwell and the House of Commons in Parliament. After a series of military conflicts, Cromwell and the Puritans won, and Charles I was beheaded in 1649. From then until 1660 England was ruled as a Commonwealth by Cromwell as Lord Protector. A stripped-down Parliament (with no House of Lords) was included in the plan but actually had very little power or even ability among its members to rule. Cromwell's entourage included the Reverend Hugh Peters as chaplain, who had returned from Salem in 1641 as a member of the Massachusetts Bay Colony's trading commission and then became a close friend and advisor to Cromwell.

Marblehead's first settlement occurred about 1629. Until 1634 the place was mainly a "fishing station" with residents coming from several directions. First were the fishermen sent from England by Governor Matthew Craddock, who held the right to develop the fishing resources as far as the English authorities were concerned. These fishermen and seamen, who spent more time at sea than they did in their crude, grass-roofed huts ashore, were joined by other fishermen from Salem and the surrounding area. Many of these were people who simply could not abide with the strict Puritan rules imposed by Salem authorities. The town's mission was fishing, and this was intended to turn a profit for Craddock and the other investors in England. In return, Craddock supplied boats and rudimentary fishing equipment. Poor in material goods and surrounded by a frequently hostile environment, the real goal of most Marbleheaders in these early times was simple survival.

The fishermen were shortly joined by a small number of resident owners of boats for fishing and trade. Representative of these was Isaac Allerton, an entrepreneur who first came to the colonies on the *Mayflower* in 1620. Allerton had built a reputation for freewheeling financial dealing and rather more concern for personal profit, vis-à-vis that of the community, than the Plymouth authorities could countenance. He arrived in Marblehead around 1633 and began to build what might have been the one real success of his life. In 1634 Governor John Winthrop's journal tells of a fire in "Governor Craddock's house" from which Allerton and several fishermen in his employ miraculously escaped.

Unfortunately, Allerton was not so lucky in his dealings with the General Court in Boston, which acted as the governing body for the Massachusetts Bay Colony. In the early spring of 1635 he was called to receive the General Court's banishment from the colony. In May he conveyed all his property to his son-in-law, Moses Maverick, and resettled in Connecticut, where he died several years later in poverty.

Isaac Allerton had left two seeds that contributed immeasurably to Marblehead's development. The fishing venture he founded had started to show signs of success, with eight boats operating and a ready market in England for the produce. And in 1635 he had sent a shallop (a type of small boat) to Newbury to pick up the Reverend John Avery, who had agreed to come with his family to be Marblehead's minister. As previously mentioned, the boat ran into a violent nor'easter off Cape Ann, was blown aground on an island, and the Avery family perished. However, Marblehead's need for a minister continued and grew and the diversity of her citizens demanded independence from any one sect.

Salem records of 1638 show a grant "To Mr. Walton, [of] eight acres on the Main." "Mr. Walton" was William Walton, Marblehead's first minister, who was destined to serve the town for thirty years without ordination by the Congregational Church. Born in Somerset, England, he earned a bachelor's degree from Emmanuel College, Cambridge, in 1621 and a master's degree in 1625. He was ordained an Anglican minister at Seaton, England, almost immediately afterward and settled into a comfortable ministry there. In 1628 he married Elizabeth Cooke. Their first two children, Elizabeth and John, were born in England. In 1633 Walton sailed from England to Hingham, Massachusetts.

The reasons for his departure were almost certainly political. King Charles I had continued his father's policy of enforcing strongly a High Church theology and order of service in the Anglican church, and around 1633 had declared that any clergy who failed to carry out the prescribed order of worship would be imprisoned. This would certainly be intolerable for a clergyman who believed in any local church autonomy at all or, for that matter, any participation by the laity in liturgical or theological matters.

Marker erected in 1930 by the Massachusetts Bay Colony Tercentenary Commission.

No direct statement of Walton's politics or philosophy exists today. He apparently was not closely involved with the Puritan movement in England, and was certainly no Separatist. Nevertheless, Charles's edicts would have been more than sufficient to drive him away. It seems most likely that Walton became what we would today call a nondenominational, liberal clergyman.

There was already a minister in Hingham when he arrived, so William Walton taught school there for two or three years. Then, apparently in 1637, he was called to Marblehead as a "missionary" to the fishermen and other residents there.

Whether or not he headed an "organized" church, the minister held a key position in colonial life at the time of Walton's arrival in Marblehead. The vast majority of residents were illiterate; even the few "gentry" such as Moses Maverick and John Humphrey lacked the formal education that Mr. Walton had. The minister was thus not only the preacher but also a teacher and an ambassador in the townspeople's communications with colonial authorities. The minister was the town's only paid officer: for his first year in Marblehead, Mr. Walton received forty pounds — paid, more often than not, in fish or other goods. Finally, with so few people living in town, Mr. Walton undoubtedly served a personal function, too, as a friend, advisor, and advocate in practically every human matter to any resident who needed him.

During the earliest years of William Walton's ministry, Marblehead was legally a part of Salem. The Puritan church in Salem at the time was headed by Roger Williams's successor, the Reverend Hugh Peters, and was the seat of both civil and ecclesiastical government of the extended town. Formal functions reserved for the church and its officers included not only the religious sacraments of communion, baptism, and marriage but also civil duties such as law enforcement; settlement of disputes among settlers; and granting of lands, boundaries, and pasturage. Any authorized agent of the church must be a "freeman" — a person eligible to vote and hold public office, but no one could become a freeman unless he was a church member.

For reasons both political and practical, no Marbleheaders had opted to become freemen, so the settlers there had to travel to Salem to receive church sacraments or to participate in civil functions. This meant either a tortuous overland hike along shoreline Indian trails — quite possibly a two-day journey — or a boat trip across Salem Harbor. (A ferryboat was established later with a fare of twopence and the requirement that able-bodied passengers help with the rowing!)

Marblehead's isolation from Salem led naturally to close cooperation among the residents, which gradually grew into an informal de facto system of local government. Early prominent citizens whose names appear in petitions to the Salem court or the Massachusetts General Court include William Walton, Moses Maverick, John Peach, Samuel Doliber, John Coite, and John Devereux. All the early petitions were written in William Walton's fine Cambridge hand, and his signature was invariably the first one on the document. The records that still survive deal mostly with three concerns: land allocations, defense, and the desire of Marblehead to be recognized as a town independent of Salem. Gradually, the people's objectives were met. By 1640 the Salem authorities had made their final land grants in Marblehead, recognizing the occupants' rights to hold and improve "all such lands near adjoining them as have not been formerly granted to other men."

In 1644 Marblehead's first constable was appointed. David Curwithin, who was *not* a freeman, was named by the Salem court to keep order in the town. It was the first time Marblehead had a recognized civil authority of its own. Considering the freewheeling nature of its nautical residents, this was probably long overdue.

In the same year the court granted Marblehead the right to build a fort overlooking Salem Harbor on Peach's Point. Two guns would be the colony's contribution to this effort.

Finally, in 1648-49, the General Court completed the process of mak-

Plaque at Old Burial Hill commemorating construction of the First Meeting House.

ing Marblehead a separate town. From that time on Marblehead would govern itself through its own town meeting process. William Walton and his successors would have a vital role in the process, as the church was to remain a central institution in colonial life for another century and more. That Marblehead's church was markedly different in character from those of Salem, Plymouth, Boston, or other towns was only a natural extension of the character of the town's residents and their needs.

During the early years Marblehead's development was spurred on by its population growth through immigration and by the success and growth of its fishing industry. An economy that was almost entirely based on barter in the early 1630s was to develop into a healthy, largely cash system later in the century. From 1630 to 1641 more immigrants came to the colonies from Europe than in all the succeeding years up to the Revolution. Marblehead received its share of these immigrants. In addition to the fishermen, around whose trade the town's economy developed, there were tradesmen, shipbuilders, men of commerce, and — of course — tavernkeepers.

The fishing industry was the heart of Marblehead's economy and has been cited in several historical accounts as one reason why the early colonial powers were willing to countenance the differences in philosophy and lifestyle that made Marblehead uniquely "rough and tumble" among the towns. Simply, fish were Massachusetts Bay's most profitable export, and Marblehead's fisheries were more successful than those of any other town. Fishing was done by hand line or net from a number of small boats plying the coastal waters. The day's catch was brought in, cleaned, heavily salted, and laid out to sun-dry on wooden racks called stages or flakes. By means of salting and drying, cod, haddock, halibut, mackerel, and other fish could be preserved for the time needed to accumulate and transport the fish in shipload lots to England. Processing was done by the fishermen's wives and children while the men were out catching more fish. It was hard, dirty work. The preserved fish, though, were a rich and economical protein source for England's food markets. From all reports, the size and quantity of fish available off the North Shore made much larger yields possible than at any other location. Good profits were available for those willing to work hard enough to earn them.

Shipbuilding was another early venture of Marbleheaders. In 1636 the 120-ton *Desire* was built at Salem Harbor, where Naugus Head is now. This was the third ship built in the colonies and was captained by William Pierce, a close associate of Isaac Allerton and Matthew Craddock. The

Desire set a new record for an ocean crossing — twenty-three days to Gravesend, England. She carried large, profitable fish cargoes and was the pride of the Marblehead seagoing community. She was also involved in a famous raid on the hostile Pequot Indians at Block Island that wiped out their tribe and terrorized the rest of the Indians in the area into submission. Captain Pierce was killed in an engagement with a Spanish galleon in 1640, and the ship seems to have faded from history afterward.

Other town residents included traditional craftsmen — it was a tailor, working late at night, who discovered the fire in Craddock's house and warned Isaac Allerton and his fishermen in time to escape — and a handful of trades unique to the new community. In particular, there was a keeper of the common lands where the villagers' animals were pastured during the day. Cows had to be milked and turned over to the herdsmen by a certain hour of the morning or the owner would be responsible for any damages caused by his animals on the way to the commons.

The granting of Marblehead's petitions for recognition as a town independent of Salem, first by Salem in 1648 and then by the General Court in the spring of 1649, imposed an obligation on the residents to get the town's civic affairs in order. This was done in the first recorded town meeting, December 22, 1648. Significantly, Mr. Walton's salary of forty pounds a year was one of the first items established, along with the appointment of two men, James Smith and Joseph Doliber, to gather it. A rate was also set to provide for the meetinghouse, and an additional eigh-

Pew from the Franklin Street Church incorporating part of an original pew from the First Meeting House.

teen pence was added to each man's rate for Mr. Walton's wood.

Subsequent growth of the town can in part be traced by enlargement of the meetinghouse and by advances in Mr. Walton's salary. In 1658 this was increased to seventy pounds and thereafter varied from sixty to eighty pounds, probably according to the town's fortunes. Mr. Walton made an annual accounting of his receipts, which were still partly in goods. Samuel Roads's *History and Traditions of Marblehead* quotes some of these interesting accounts: "By half a cow of Mr. Brown, £2 2s. 6d., by 1/2 ton of mackrell, £5; by Richard Rowland in pork, £2; by Smith in cheese, 13 shillings; by Christo. Codner in liquor, 15 shillings."

The town meetinghouse, which served as both church and site of town meetings, was erected shortly after Mr. Walton's arrival on the high, rocky "burial hill" that remains to this day (Old Burial Hill). Improvements appear in the record frequently during the years from 1636 to 1683. In 1659 the town meeting "voted to have the meeting house sealed." This probably meant that churchgoers would sit in an enclosed building for the first time. The work was done by carpenter John Norman for the sum of nineteen pounds. In March 1662 the town contracted to build a gallery at the southwest corner of the meetinghouse "sufficient for 4 seats, with columns . . . stairs and other necessaries." The cost was twenty-one pounds in goods, which would be supplied during the construction as needed, with the balance to be paid in mackerel when the job was finished. In 1669 a second gallery was added at the northeast end to seat five additional people.

Finally, in 1672, a lento addition measuring 20 by 40 feet was made to the back of the meetinghouse. This evidently caused a great controversy over who would sit where in the enlarged house, and a commission was appointed to settle the matter, consisting of four of Marblehead's oldest and most respected citizens: Moses Maverick, John Devereux, John Peach, Sr., and Nicholas Merritt. A great town celebration accompanied the "raising" of the addition, leading to charges paid for rum and "fish with wine" of £4 2s. 6d.

Unlike Salem, Marblehead stayed isolated from the political events that caused civil upheaval in England and prominently involved the Puritan church. In 1660 word came that Hugh Peters, who had left Salem in 1641 and eventually joined Oliver Cromwell as his chaplain, had been executed in the wake of the English monarchy's return as King Charles II took the throne.

Marblehead's church, while it took the Puritan style of worship, was molded to meet the diverse needs of its members. Most notable was the apparent tolerance of drinking, fighting, and other "wild" behavior that would have been strictly proscribed by the traditional Puritan church. There are no notes of "fire-and-damnation" sermons by the Reverend Mr. Walton; clearly, his ministry must have taken a quieter and more beneficent course, probably based on a personal relationship with each parishioner.

He was not without his detractors, though. One citizen, Elizabeth Legg, was called into court to answer charges of slandering the minister and disorderly conduct in the meetinghouse on the Lord's day. Her confession, recorded in the Essex County Court Records, reads: "I, Elizabeth Legg doe acknowledge that I did evil and sinful in speaking slitely and scornfully of Mr. Walton and in particular in saying, I could have a boy from College that would preach better than Mr. Walton for half the wages." Mrs. Legg was sentenced to make public acknowledgment and to sit one hour in the public stocks for that offense. Another townsman, Henry Coomes, was later fined and whipped for saying that Mr. Walton "preached nothing but lies." There was, after all, a limit to the establishment's tolerance.

In October 1668 William Walton died after thirty years of service to the early Marbleheaders. Roads's account in *History and Traditions of Marblehead* sums up his ministry:

Coming [to Marblehead] as a missionary to preach the gospel he became, without ordination as a clergyman, a loving pastor, a faithful friend, and a wise and prudent counselor. His advice was sought on all matters of public or private importance, and when obtained was usually followed without question. That his loss was felt as a public bereavement by the entire community there can be little doubt.

Fortunately for the congregation, the Reverend Mr. Walton was succeeded by another man who was destined to be remembered as equally influential and dedicated in guiding the early life and growth of the church.

3

Samuel Cheever
Organizes the Church

THE 1660s saw Massachusetts experience dramatic changes in social groupings, church structure, and political policy. There had been an influx of immigrants who did not belong to the established church and who thus were not qualified as freemen. The older Puritan clergy who settled the Massachusetts Bay Colony were dying. Newer and younger clergy demanded liberalization of church law and, in the Synods of 1657, 1662, and 1664, pushed the development of the Half-Way Covenant, which entitled church members to transmit baptism (membership) rights to their children but withheld the sacraments from them.

The peninsula of Marblehead may have been somewhat isolated geographically, but its social, religious, and political policies followed those of the rest of Massachusetts. Upon the death of William Walton in 1668, the "Church on the Old Hill" issued a call for a new pastor. The summons was for a clergyman who would minister and preach to the local congregation but who, at the same time, would be subject to the strict jurisdiction of the Salem church for sacraments and for policy.

Samuel Cheever, a 1659 graduate of Harvard College, received the invitation to come to Marblehead. It was not by accident that he answered that call. Walton, an educated liberal pastor, had prepared the way for a man such as Cheever, "a man of great classick learning, a good preacher, a thorough Christian, and a prudent man." In October 1668 Cheever visited the town, and, encouraged by the independence and ruggedness of the townspeople and pushed by Salem and Boston clergy, he accepted the mantle of pastor in November.

Cheever was aided in the preparation for his calling by a family which possessed education and faith. His father, Ezekiel Cheever (1616-1708), was the author of Latin texts and almanacs and the noted schoolmaster of Boston Latin School. His mother, Mary who died in 1649 or 1650, was a very pious person and the mother of twelve children. Samuel, their eldest son, was born on September 22, 1639, and was baptized on November 15, 1639, at New Haven, Connecticut. From there, the family moved to Ipswich, Charlestown, and, lastly, to Boston.

Primary education at his father's school enabled Cheever to enter Harvard College. There he received classical training for the service of God. He graduated in good company — Nathaniel Saltonstall, later deputy to the General Court and witchcraft trial judge; Samuel Alcock, a Boston physician; Samuel Willard, pastor at the Old South Church, Boston; Samuel Belcher, pastor at Newbury; James Noyes, minister at Stonington, Connecticut; and Moses Noyes, minister at Lyme, Connecticut. After graduation Samuel remained in Boston and, in 1661, followed in his father's footsteps by publishing an almanac.

After accepting the 1668 Marblehead call, Cheever seems to have made a smooth transition from the Boston urban community to small-town life on the coast. He immediately became involved in the political and religious affairs of Marblehead. He accepted the town vote of an annual salary of forty pounds, and within a month he was the second person to sign the town petition to the crown against "imposts" (imports). From that time on he was placed in a high position of trust and was asked to witness deeds, inventories, and wills.

By tradition Cheever first lived on Gerry Island and later became a neighbor of Moses Maverick. According to the town records of 1670 a horse pasture of two acres in the lower division was laid out by Maverick, Thomas Pitman, John Peach, Jr., and John Legg, Jr., "that Mr. Cheever was to enjoy the land for a pasture on the back side of the Meeting House during his life with us and after his decease the fence to be ordered and what it shall be then with his successors to be paid for it."

Expansion of both home and pasture was necessary, for, on June 28, 1671, Cheever married Ruth Angier (1657-1742), the daughter of Edmund Angier and Ruth Ames and the granddaughter of Professor William Ames, D.D. The Cheevers eventually had ten children, one of whom was the Reverend Ames Cheever, the first minister at Manchester, Massachusetts.

The town meeting recognized the needs of the pastor's rapidly growing family, and his salary was increased to eighty pounds in country pay and in cash.

As previously mentioned, in 1672 a "lento" with three gabled ends was added to the church. In typical Massachusetts fashion this addition created a controversy over the question of seating in the expanded section. Pastoral tenderness and the advice of a committee solved this problem.

In 1678, as the pastor's family grew, so did the demand for solid cash. The town meeting of that year granted Cheever a salary of seventy pounds in hard currency. By 1682 it was increased to seventy-five pounds in cash.

Tranquility, never a permanent state in Massachusetts, was shattered during the years 1682-84. Colonial politics reflected conflicts between the English colonials and the moderate New Englanders and between the scolding royal mother country and the young Congregational colony. By early 1684 word was received that the charter of the Massachusetts Bay Colony had been suspended, that the General Court had been dismissed, and that Massachusetts had been made a royal colony under an appointed governor. In addition, local problems concerning town financial accounting, mounting fear that land grants issued by the General Court would be in jeopardy, and pressing Indian land claims to the town all stirred an already bubbling pot. Greater fear that royal control would change the existing voting franchise and the tax support of the Congregational churches pushed the colonists to action.

Acts of defiance, faith, and the demand for independence from the new government combined when the Marblehead church members moved to gain local autonomy on May 24, 1684. Fifty parishioners presented their names on a petition requesting the First Church in Salem to grant them with their children a dismissal to become a church separate from all others. In their pleas for separation, they indicated "a great inconveniency in going to Salem" and asked that Samuel Cheever "who had been their minister fifteen years and a half to take the office of a Pastor and themselves might be congregated into a particular society for ye enjoyment of all the ordinances in this place as in other Towns and places in the country." The Salem church received their petition on June 6, 1684, and most likely granted separation immediately after that date.

On July 6, after "serious advice and deliberation," the Marblehead congregation voted to form together and to request Cheever to be ordained. He "expressed his willingness to serve his generation by the will of God, and to give up himself to that particular service, so long as peaceably and with a good conscience, according to his best knowledge of the mind of

God in his word he could discharge such an office among them."

The town then proceeded on its own course of independence. Political action followed on July 14 when Marblehead purchased the land from the Indian claimants, thus protecting their ownership and voting rights. Immediate town action appointed a committee, of which Cheever was a member, "to proportion each Man's part according to his privilege in the township" and thus forestalled any conflict between the old "commoners" and new settlers.

In preparation for separation on July 16, a fast was conducted in Marblehead by the Reverend John Hale of Beverly, "calling in the help and advice of the neighboring churches, by their elders and messengers, viz Salem, Ipswich, Lynn, and Beverly." The creation of the First Church of Christ of Marblehead came on August 13, 1684, in the "Church on the Old Hill." On that day, fifty-four Christians placed their names upon a confession of faith and upon a church covenant. Their actions marked more than a desire for political power or local autonomy. Their sincere efforts were a clear statement of their belief in Jesus Christ, of their trust in the future, and of their desire for independence. Those believers pledged "to keep themselves pure" and "to observe the Lord's commands thus walking together as a particular church of Christ, in all ways of his worship and service, according to the rules of the word of God." As they promised "to watch over one another's souls," their names, which are listed in the appendices, still stand as a testimony of that brotherly love.

Those members then witnessed the ordination of their beloved pastor of almost sixteen years, Samuel Cheever. That solemn event was performed

Foot warmer which was in use in Old North up through the 1800s.

Sketch of the First Meeting House on Old
Burial Hill as it appeared in 1684.

by the Reverend John Higginson of the Salem church, who gave the charge;
by the Reverend Mr. Hubbard of the Ipswich Parish, who extended the
right hand of fellowship; and by the Reverend John Hale of the Beverly
church, who with the above pastors concluded with the "laying on of
hands" upon Cheever. The civil authorities of the Massachusetts Bay Colony were represented by the deputy governor, Thomas Danforth; five
assistants; and twenty elders. Immediately, on August 30, 1684, the
Reverend Mr. Cheever and the parish issued a call for the baptism of the
children of the church members.

A decision was reached that the sacrament of the Lord's Supper would
be administered to the faithful on the first Sabbath of each month. The
formal organization of the church body came with the election of two
deacons — Benjamin Gale and Richard Reith. By September the church
records indicate that there had been more baptisms and that additional
citizens had signed the covenant. The first priestly duties of the newly
ordained minister came on October 5, 1684, when Cheever administered
the first Lord's Supper in Marblehead. Recognition of the new pastor also
came in that year when he was asked to deliver the election sermon in

Boston based upon Hebrews 2 : 10 to the Ancient and Honorable Artillery Company.

Unfortunately, hard times soon fell upon the Congregational pastors in Massachusetts with the 1686 Dominion government of the royal governor, Edmund Andros. The cash flow to the Marblehead pastor's salary was restricted, as town records of 1701 read: "Mr. Samuel Cheevers be allowed ffower [sic] pounds 18.6 for trepass in the Comans the last two years and to be accompted as soe much pd him for amt of the Town for his service in the yeares of Sir Edmund Andros government when no rate was made." By 1689, with the Glorious Revolution in England, the Dominion government in New England was overthrown. After pledging loyalty to the new monarchs, William and Mary, the Congregational pastors in the Boston area formed the first Ministerial Association in 1690.

With the unification of the coastal Congregational pastors controlling church policy and the success of the provincial assembly in overturning royal authority, Massachusetts citizens began to have a more positive outlook. However, events were happening which would quickly change what the citizens thought was an ideal life. The deposed royal governor was replaced by a new non-Puritan governor. War broke out with the Indians, and problems surfaced between colonists and the French. Taxes were raised, and the citizens of Massachusetts Bay experienced a particularly cruel winter.

Further, the religious community was alarmed by a serious affliction which descended upon the North Shore in 1692. There, a small group of unmarried young girls and women in Salem Village (present-day Danvers) complained that the influence of the Evil One was upon them. The infamous witch hysteria had begun.

To combat the powers of darkness, the local clergy, headed by the Reverend Cotton Mather, the Reverend John Hale, and the Reverend Deodat Lawson, rushed to the isolated community of the Reverend Samuel Parris. Prayers and preaching failed to stem the forces of witchcraft. Cries against the aged, deformed, nonconformers, and the "different" filled Essex County. When the hysteria finally ended, 19 men and women had been hanged for the crime; 1 man had been crushed to death for refusal to enter a plea; and nearly 150 citizens had been left in prison, either condemned to death or awaiting trial. Historians have claimed that feuds, land disputes, personal jealousy, church politics, superstition, "power plays" between towns, hatred, religious fervor, and isolation were among the many causes for the tragic affair.

With the rest of Essex County actively accusing and condemning,

Tombstones in the graveyard on Old Burial Hill.

Marblehead maintained its independence from Salem, remaining away from the hysteria, except for the execution of one townsperson and the imprisonment of a former citizen of the town. Credit must be given to the strong, quiet leadership of the Reverend Samuel Cheever. For, surrounded by Salem Village which accused twenty-nine, "Salem Towne" with ten, Beverly with ten, and Lynn with nine, Marblehead lost only one to the fervor of the times.

Three years after the mass hysteria, the First Church in Marblehead found that it had outgrown the old meetinghouse on the hill, which is now called the Old Burial Hill. At the town meeting of March 25, 1695, the community voted that Capt. Nathaniel Norden, Erasmus James, and John Browne were "chosen to get the peoples voluntary gifts and see subscribers for and toward the Building of a meetinghouse and to make returns to the next Towne meeting of their proceedings that Care may be farther taken for the work."

On April 10, 1695, the men reported a list of 163 "well disposed Christians" who had pledged to the building fund. By September 16, 60 more citizens contributed to raise the amount pledged to £586 15s. A formal committee composed of Capt. John Legg (chairman), John Browne (clerk), Capt. Nathaniel Norden, Ambrose Gale, Sr., Richard Reith, Eleazor Ingols, Richard Grosse, and John Waldron, Sr., was created to supervise the building of the structure and to seat the parishioners. The building located on Franklin Street ("fifty-three feet long, forty-seven feet broad, twenty foot studd") would serve as the First Church from 1695 until the congregation relocated to its present structure on Washington Street.

Because the new structure had been oversubscribed, the materials from the old church were used to build a schoolhouse. To supply the post of schoolmaster, the Reverend Mr. Cheever recommended the settlement of Mr. Josiah Cotton, the grandson of the Reverend John Cotton. His salary was set at fifteen pounds annually, and he lived with the Marblehead pastor. Encouraged by Cheever, Josiah Cotton preached his first sermon on November 23, 1701. After furthering the education of the community's children with his excellent skills, Cotton left Marblehead in 1704.

Samuel Cheever's own skill as an orator and the respect accorded him by his fellow clergy led to his being invited to preach the provincial election sermon in Boston on May 28, 1712. This sermon was entitled "God's Sovereign Government Among the Nations" (based on Psalms 95 : 3-6 and 2 : 12) and was published at the expense of the Massachusetts Council.

Cheever continued his parish duties, but advancing age began to hamper his efforts. In 1714 the town decided to summon a colleague to aid him. Three candidates were selected: Mr. Edward Holyoke; Mr. Ames Cheever, the pastor's son; and Mr. John Barnard. The election of Barnard in 1715 and his ordination on July 18, 1716, as copastor led to a dispute and later to the creation of the Second Church under Holyoke.

In the thirty-two years that Cheever ministered alone to the First Church (1684-1716), he admitted 41 males and 160 females to membership; 345 persons to recognition of the covenant; and 1,557 persons to baptism. For three more years after 1716 Cheever preached, and Barnard carried out the day-to-day duties of the pastor.

In one of his last sermons (October 1719), Cheever saw the end of his service in Marblehead:

I must work the works of him that sent me, while it is day; the night cometh, when no man can work. . . . Age is too heavy for me, but I must bear it. I cannot die when I would. I must wait patiently God's time. My times are in his hands. I rejoice that he has provided for his people before I go. He has satisfied me with long life.

Barnard wrote of the elder priest, who was then the oldest graduate of Harvard:

At upwards of fourscore, he could read without the help of spectacles and had his Hearing quick as Youth to the last week of His Life; but the Powers of his Mind, some few years before he died, failed, especially his Memory, whereby he was greatly unfitted even for common Conversation; and yet his constant Family Prayers, were orderly and regular; so did Grace shine in the decays of Nature. . . . His Lamp of Life fairly burning out, without being put out; for he felt no Sickness nor pain to the last.

Barnard respected the old pastor as "an owner of solid judgement, a copious Invention, and a tenancious Memory" who "had an uncommon Knowledge in the holy Scripture, being an excellent Text-man." The Reverend Samuel Dana wrote of Cheever, "The whole tenour of his life evinced an entire submission to the disposing Providence of God and acquiescense in it. His deportment was uniform, blameless, and exemplary."

With a firm faith, the Reverend Samuel Cheever entered into eternal rest on May 29, 1724. He was buried on the rise of the Old Burying Ground not far from, if not on the exact location of, the pulpit of the old meetinghouse.

To his memory, a grateful parish erected a stone with an appropriate Latin inscription, which reads:

With this sod are covered the remains of Mr. Samuel Cheever, the Reverend Pastor of the first Church of our Lord Jesus Christ in Marblehead. At the time of his decease, though he had entered his 85th year, he possessed almost the vigour of youth, and scarcely appeared to have grown old. He discharged the pastoral duties toward the flock of the Great Shepard, with the greatest integrity, diligence, and watchfulness, in love, benevolence, and affection, for 50 years; until spent with his labours, he was confined about four years to his dwelling, still zealously devoting himself to his studies and prayer, while his people deeply lamented his loss, though it was so remarkably supplied. At length, his work being done, and, with perfect resignation, without pain, with no disease but mere age, he departed, and sweetly slept in Jesus.

4

Parson John Barnard

PARSON JOHN BARNARD was minister of the First Church from 1715 to 1770, a period of fifty-four years. During the first eight years he served as assistant to the Reverend Samuel Cheever, who was then a very old man.

Parson Barnard's life and personality have always been of great interest, since his influence was not limited to the First Church but included Marblehead and the provinces of New England. In his history historian Samuel Roads quotes Dr. Charles W. Eliot of Harvard as saying that Barnard was "a burning and shining light for many years and his praise was in all the churches. He seemed like a high priest among the clergy."

A large part of this chapter is based on Parson Barnard's *Autobiography*, written in his old age at the request of his friend, the Reverend Dr. Ezra Stiles, president of Yale College. The *Autobiography* is widely quoted by historians, since it gives an authentic firsthand description of life in Massachusetts when it was a British province, and of the friendly contacts with the mother country before the unpleasantness concerning taxation without representation had become a burning issue.

Some thought should be given to the period of history in which John Barnard lived. Boston was a thriving colonial seaport with some fine homes. Harvard College was a little more than sixty years old at the time of Barnard's graduation. The royal governor of Massachusetts had sworn allegiance to Queen Anne, but her throne was none too secure because Prince James III was constantly expected to invade England from France in an attempt to take the power which had been bitterly contested by

The Parson Barnard House.

Catholics and Protestants since the beheading of Charles I. The War of
the Spanish Succession was raging in Europe with repercussions in North
America. This was followed by the Seven Years' War, which in North
America became the French and Indian War.

John Barnard lived in a period of great growth in the colonies where
there was an increasing spirit of self-determination and independence. He
had a real influence on the life and thought of the people, as will be seen
as this account progresses.

Born in Boston in 1681, John Barnard completed his grammar school
education in that city and entered Harvard College when he was not quite
fifteen years old. Dr. Increase Mather was then president of the college.
In 1700, when nearly nineteen years of age, Barnard graduated with
honors. At that time he had come to the realization "that the pulpit was
his great design and divinity was his chief study." Therefore, he joined
the North Church (Congregational) in Boston and began his studies for
the ministry at Harvard.

There was a society of young men which gathered in homes on Sunday evenings for religious worship and to practice preaching. To them

John Barnard preached his first sermon. By 1703 he had become a "constant" preacher and received the degree of master of arts from Harvard.

During the years 1704 and 1705 Barnard served the church in Yarmouth, Massachusetts, as an assistant to one of the famous Cotton family, Dr. John Cotton, who had become old and feeble.

In 1707 the War of the Spanish Succession had spread from Europe to the colonies, and Governor Joseph Dudley of Massachusetts tried to force the French residents of Nova Scotia to obedience to the crown of England. Two Massachusetts regiments were sent to Nova Scotia to capture a well-garrisoned fort located at Annapolis Royal. Barnard served as chaplain in one regiment. The Massachusetts regiments encountered a series of reverses and returned home without capturing the French fort.

In the summer of 1709 Barnard was appointed chaplain on a British warship which sailed first to Barbados Island and then to England where he stayed for about eleven months. Barnard arrived there with letters of introduction from friends of his father and Boston clergymen and was able to participate in eighteenth-century English life.

Talents and education seldom go unnoticed, and Barnard's made a great impression on the British. He preached frequently in the Puritan churches, whose members were then known in England as the Dissenters. He tells with pride that on one occasion he preached to "a great concourse of the Scotch nobility and gentry."

During this time in England Barnard was invited to be chaplain to the British lord lieutenant, who was going to serve in Ireland as the queen's representative. This appointment would have required that he become a member of the established church of England, and he could not conscientiously subscribe to the Thirty-Nine Articles of the established church, thus proving that he was a loyal Dissenter of firm faith. However, he attended an Episcopal church to hear the bishop and receive his blessing.

Home again, Barnard resumed preaching in pulpits in and around Boston. On May 4, 1713, Cotton Mather wrote in his diary, "some gentleman from Marblehead desires me to make a visit to that place." On July 8 Mr. Mather wrote that he was "proposing a journey to Marblehead," and on July 12 he recorded he had preached in the First Church and noted, "If their aged minister, Mr. Cheever, dies before another minister and a good and wise and faithful one be settled among them, there will be extreme Hazards of their falling into miserable confusion."

However, it was not until August 1714 that John Barnard, Edward Holyoke, and Amos Cheever were invited to preach alternately to the congregation for three months on probation. In January 1715 the church "came

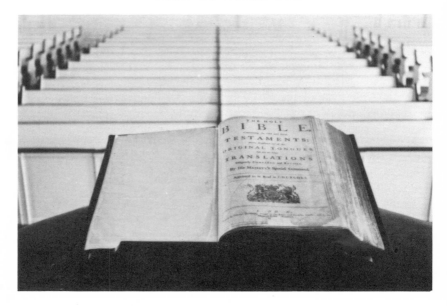

The Parson Barnard bible on the lectern of Old North.

to a choice," and that choice was John Barnard. The town concurred in it and voted a salary.

Now Mr. Barnard knew that there were "two of the church and some chief men of the town who would prefer Mr. Holyoke." He did not want to begin with internal problems, so he inquired if the town was large enough to require another "house." The response was yes.

Mr. Barnard agreed to accept the call to the First Church, and Mr. Holyoke agreed to form a second church. Four men and twenty-four women requested dismissal to form the Second Congregational Church.

On November 1715 Mr. Barnard began his duties with Mr. Cheever and was ordained on July 18, 1716, three years after Cotton Mather had pointed out the need for "a good and wise and faithful" man, which criteria he certainly met. Rev. Samuel Cheever retired a few years later. Holyoke and Barnard worked together in harmony and friendship for twenty years.

Thus began Parson Barnard's long and distinguished ministry to the First Church and his service to the whole town. Of his ordination ceremony, historian Samuel Roads said in his history, "as the smiles of Providence were seen in the temperateness of the day, so the solemnity was countenanced with the presence of several councilors, many ministers, and a vast assembly of people from all parts." The ordination sermon was preached by Dr. Cotton Mather.

The First Church had moved from Old Burial Hill to the second meetinghouse on Franklin Street some years before Barnard came to Marblehead. Three years after he arrived, Barnard married Miss Anna Woodbury of Ipswich. In his *Autobiography* he said of her, "she was a young gentlewoman of comely personage and good fortune, and above all strictly virtuous and of admirable economy." There is no other mention of family life in the *Autobiography*. The Barnards built a fine colonial mansion diagonally across the street from the church and furnished it with beautiful furniture, judging by pictures of some of the pieces now extant. Later this house was converted into apartments.

The marriage was not blessed with children, but Barnard records that "as one of his charities he generally kept two boys of poor parents in school, and that by this means he was instrumental in bringing up good men and valuable members of the Commonwealth."

In 1717 the first association of church clergy in Essex County was formed. Mr. Barnard mentions the business of the association as one of his duties. He took an active part in helping the churches of the association to solve their difficulties, bringing peace and harmony to the churches, and even appearing in court on behest of Cotton Mather on behalf of a minister unjustly accused.

In 1724 Barnard was invited to leave Marblehead to become one of the two ministers of the North Church in Boston. His answer, however, was as follows: "I look upon myself as being so strongly engaged to Marblehead from their kind treatment of me that no prospect of worldly interest shall prevail with me to leave them."

All evidence shows that Barnard was a mightly preacher. He kept a notebook record of the sermons he preached, listing the text of 6,000 sermons; the places and dates of delivery; and the honoraria he received, amounting to an excess of £10,000. That notebook is now in the files of the Massachusetts Historical Society. Included in the collections of Abbot Library in Marblehead and Essex Institute in Salem there is today a total of fourteen printed books of Barnard's sermons and addresses. In the files of the First Church there is one book which contains six of his sermons, titled "The Christian Hero, or the Saint's Victory and Rewards."

In 1734 Parson Barnard went to Boston to preach an election sermon to the royal governor and his Council. The representatives of the General Court were also present.

In 1737 the president of Harvard College died. Some of the college overseers proposed to Barnard that he accept the presidency of the college. However, Barnard considered that he had been out of touch with the academic world for too long a period, so he suggested that the college consider the Reverend Edward Holyoke of the Second Congregational Church for that office. Holyoke had lived at Harvard for fourteen years, serving as a tutor there for most of that time. When the invitation was first extended to the Reverend Mr. Holyoke, the members of his church "voted not to part with him." When the college extended a second invitation to accept the presidency, his Marblehead church asked Parson Barnard to open their meeting with prayer to guide their deliberations, and the Second Church membership voted to release Holyoke from his ministry to them. After he left for Cambridge some people asked members of his church "how they were persuaded to part with so valuable a man." In answer they replied, "Old Barnard prayed him away."

In 1756 Parson Barnard accepted an invitation to deliver a sermon at the Harvard College chapel under a lecture foundation established from a legacy given by Massachusetts Chief Justice Dudley. Invitations to preach before such distinguished groups were considered an honor greatly to be desired.

The Rev. William Bentley of Salem, whose comments in his diary were often caustic, referred to Parson Barnard as "the Bishop of the place." Another contemporary described Parson Barnard as follows: "His countenance was grand, his mien majestic, and there was a dignity in his whole deportment. His presence restrained every imprudence and folly of youth, and when the aged saw him they arose and stood up." Still another said of him, "his charity was worthy of imitation, the poor were often fed, the widows' hearts sang with joy, but knew not where to return thanks except to God."

In a lecture given before the Massachusetts Historical Society in 1896, the speaker described Parson Barnard in the following words: "He was eminent in both learning and piety and was famous among the divines of America. He was an accomplished scholar in Greek, Latin, and Hebrew and in mathematics. His amusement was naval architecture, and his models were highly commended."

Parson Barnard said that his Marblehead church had once or twice been thrown into a controversy and that, although he had some of the chief and most stubborn spirits to deal with, they had, for more than fifty years, enjoyed as great peace and unity as any church in the country.

For a time Barnard was paid in paper currency which was greatly depreciated. When silver replaced paper currency, a committee from the

Early view of a Marblehead fish flake or fence for drying cod and haddock.

church waited on the parson and asked him how much his pay was short: it was found to be £740. Barnard declined to accept any reimbursement and said, "I sought not their substance but them."

There were many evidences of Parson Barnard's generosity, one of which was the gift of a beautiful silver tankard to the First Church to be used for the communion service, one of the church's cherished possessions. The pulpit Bible, given by Parson Barnard's brother, is still in use. It was printed in London in 1754 in the ancient type with the F's and S's which can confuse a modern reader.

Although unwilling to become president, Parson Barnard retained his interest in, and loyalty to, Harvard College throughout his life. When the Harvard Library burned in 1764, he presented to the college many books from his own library and others which he purchased from England.

Following is an excerpt from his Autobiography:

When I came, there was not so much as one proper carpenter, mason, tailor, nor butcher in the town, nor anything of a market worth mentioning; but they had their homes built by country workmen, and their clothes made out of town, and they supplied themselves with beef and pork from Boston, which drained the town of its money. But now we abound in artificers, and some of the best, and our markets are large. And what, above all, I would remark, there was not so much as one foreign trading vessel belonging to the town. The people contented themselves to be the slaves that digged in the mines and left the merchants of Boston, Salem, and Europe to carry away the gains; by which means the town was always in dismally poor circumstances, involved in debt to the merchants, more than they were worth; nor could I find twenty families in it that could stand upon their own legs; and they were generally as rude, swearing, drunken, and fighting a crew as they were poor. Whereas, not only are the public ways mended, but the manners of the people are greatly cultivated; and we have many gentlemen-like and polite families, and the very fishermen generally scorn the rudeness of the former generation.

I soon saw the town had a price in its hands, and I, therefore, laid myself out to get acquaintance with the English masters of vessels, that I might, by them, be let into the mystery of the fish trade, and in a little time I gained a pretty thorough understanding in it. When I saw the advantages of it I thought it my duty to stir up my people to send the fish to market themselves, that they might reap the benefit of it, to the enriching of themselves and serving the town. But, alas, I could inspire no man with courage and resolution enough to engage in it till I met with Mr. Joseph Swett, a young man of strict justice, great industry, enterprising genius, quick apprehension, and firm resolution, but of small fortune. To him I opened myself fully, laid the scheme clearly before him, and he hearkened unto me, and was wise enough to put it into practice. He first sent a small cargo to Barbados. He soon found he increased his stock, built vessels, and sent the fish to Europe, and prospered in the trade to the enriching of himself. Some of his family, by carrying on the trade, have arrived at large estates. The more promising young men of the town soon followed his example; so that now we have between thirty and forty ships, brigs, snows and topsail schooners engaged in foreign trade. From so small a beginning the town has risen into its present flourishing circumstances, and we need no foreigner to transport our fish, but are able ourselves to send it all to the market.

Available records show that Marblehead did have some foreign commerce in the latter part of the seventeenth century but that these early beginnings had disappeared before Barnard came to Marblehead in 1715. So honor is due to Parson Barnard and Joseph Swett for resurrecting the foreign trade on broader and more certain base. In 1932 Hammond Bowden, former president of the Marblehead Historical Society, in a paper on foreign trade and commerce confirmed the steady growth of this shipping prior to the Revolutionary War.

One indication of the prosperity that was inspired by Barnard is of special interest. In the year 1752 a call for aid went out from the city of Boston, and at a Fast Day service in the church a collection was taken for the poor of Boston, which amounted to £166. This is in contrast to the poverty in Marblehead when Barnard arrived.

As the exporting of the dried salt codfish brought great prosperity to many families along the coast of Massachusetts Bay they became known as the "Codfish Aristocracy" of the province. In Marblehead the Lees, Hoopers, and Swetts were outstanding families in that category. In the House of Representatives in the Massachusetts State House there is a golden replica of the codfish, a fitting reminder of that early prosperity.

Captain Swett became a leading citizen of the town, and Samuel Road's *History* records him as a member of the committee appointed to erect a fortification for the defense of the harbor. That fortification was later named Fort Sewall.

Joseph Swett's granddaughters all married well. Martha Swett married Jeremiah Lee; Ruth married "King" Hooper; Hannah married Dr. Joseph Lemmon; and Sarah became the wife of Benjamin Marston, a prosperous Tory.

These descendants of Joseph Swett showed their gratitude for what John Barnard had done for them and the town by presenting some of the beautiful communion silver to the church on May 7, 1759. Joseph Swett and granddaughters Ruth Hooper and Martha Lee and grandson-in-law Dr. Lemmon gave a flagon, as did Robert Hooper, another grandson-in-law. In 1773 Dr. Lemmon gave the beautiful baptismal bowl made by Paul Revere which is used at all baptisms today.

Miss Sarah Swett's legacy which honored Parson Barnard and was received in the 1930s provided the money to restore the old pulpit which

Gravestone of John Barnard at Old Burial Hill.

had been in the church attic for fifty years and to build the beautiful reredos behind it. A silver plaque on the pulpit states that the restoration was done in memory of the beloved pastor.

In 1760 Mr. Barnard felt he needed assistance, and the church voted to provide help. On May 24, 1761, Mr. William Whitwell preached as a candidate, and after hearing him several times it was decided he was the man, and in October he was invited to come. He preached one part of each Sunday and according to Roads' *History* was ordained on August 25, 1762.

Parson Barnard wrote in his *Autobiography,* "My people are provided with a very good man, an excellent preacher, and a worthy minister, and I with a very obliging, dutiful son."

Parson Barnard had rarely been ill or away from the pulpit, but in February 1768 his sight failed. He continued to preach as long as he was able and delivered his last sermon on January 8, 1766. He died on January 24, 1770, after long, devoted service to the church and Marblehead.

In his will Mr. Barnard bequeathed £200 to Harvard College,

> to be paid after his wife's decease, into the hands of the treasurer of said college to be "improved" for the benefit of said college. It is my desire that if John Barnard Swett, now a student of said college should, after graduation, be inclined to apply himself to his studies and resides at the college, and if the 200 pounds have been received by the treasurer, he may have the benefit of the income for three years, after which it shall be "improved" without incumberance.

This showed the continuing tie between Barnard and the Swetts.

The will gave to the church the lots given to Barnard by the commoners when he came to Marblehead. This land, situated next to Judge Nathan Bowen's, was part swamp and part pastureland, and was sold in 1868 to provide money to purchase land on High Street on which to build the parsonage.

Parson Barnard ends his account of the development of Marblehead's foreign commerce with these words: "Let God have the praise, who has redeemed the town from a state of bondage into a state of liberty and freedom." As Marblehead continued to grow and prosper it became a fitting tribute and memorial to Parson Barnard's inspiration and leadership that the town was able to participate so gloriously in the Revolutionary War and in the founding of the Republic, as recounted in the following chapter.

5

The Church
and the Revolution

T HE CLOUD of apprehension and
despair was rapidly changing its
hue of lambent gray to charcoal
black on the eve of the Revolution in the decade of the 1760s. Many factors contributed to the worries and feelings of the Marbleheaders. The
rock foundation of the church itself seemed to be loosening, for the man
whose vision, leadership, and persuasion had made him the dominant
figure both in the economic as well as in the spiritual climate of the town
had announced in the beginning of the year 1760 (in his seventy-ninth
year) that his strength was failing and that the church should be searching
for his replacement. A committee was appointed, and the man of the times
(Parson John Barnard) painstakingly recorded the procedures in his
Autobiography:

We then heard some others, and among them Mr. William Whitwell, son of
Mr. William Whitwell, merchant in Boston, who preached his first sermon 24th
May, 1761. Upon several times hearing of him, my church and congregation
generally inclined to him, and thought it needless to hear any other, and therefore
soon after, that is in October, desired him to come and live among us, and carry
on the labors of the pulpit with me constantly. He did so, October 31, [1761] and
from that time preached one part of each Sabbath. The chief of my flock having
told me they relied upon me as to his principles, which they thought I was a better judge of than themselves, and, if I approved of him, they would look no farther, for fear lest, by hearing many, they should grow divided in their opinions.
I informed them that upon hearing of him, and often conversing with him, I could

not but approve of his principles; that, upon inquiry among the ministers of Boston, who knew him, I found they valued him as a serious, good man, of good learning, and of sound principles. Upon which they agreed with him to preach every other Sabbath for three months, and then desired him to move into the town, that we might be better acquainted with him. I let him know that my people grew more and more disposed to fix him among us, and there would be no hazard of his being chosen; and he came to dwell with us, as above. The 14th of January, 1762, we had a day of prayer for direction and blessing; and January 17th, we had a church meeting and unanimously chose Mr. William Whitwell for our minister; the same day the congregation met and unanimously concurred with the church's choice. When they were about to vote for his salary, they let me know that they feared it would be offensive to me if they voted him more than they gave me. Upon which, being present at their meeting, I declared to them, that it would be so far from an offense to me, that I verily thought he would need more than I had, and it would be highly pleasing to me to see them fix a better stipend upon him, especially after my decease, when they would not have the burden of two to support. Upon which they readily voted him a salary of one hundred and four pounds during my life, and an hundred sterling after my decease.

At great length and detail did the Reverend John Barnard write about the minister who would be the shepherd of the First Church during the eve of the Revolution and the war days. Mr. Whitwell brought his wife, Prudence, to the house of shoreman George Knight on High Street. Born in Boston in 1736, he brought to his ministry a college degree from Princeton. He was earnest, energetic, and a great patriot. Devoted to his calling, he treated Mr. Barnard with great respect and devotion, as is recorded in the funeral sermon he preached at Mr. Barnard's demise — the only piece of writing from Mr. Whitwell's pen that has survived the years. He was not a diarist, so that the assumption has to be that during his trial periods he went to Martha's Vineyard where he met his future wife and then later to Sandwich, Massachusetts; both trips were probably made by boat — certainly the one to Martha's Vineyard. Not only were the trials and tribulations of the colonies to try his stamina and soul, but also his personal life was to make great demands upon his understanding and patience.

His family consisted of a daughter, Prudence, baptized on November 24, 1765; another daughter, Elisabeth, baptized on December 27, 1767; and a son, Nathaniel, baptized on February 28, 1773. His wife, Prudence, probably died during childbirth with the arrival of Nathaniel, for her death at "age 33" is recorded as of February 1773. It was the custom of the times for widowers to remarry after a short period of time. Thus, Mr. Whitwell traveled to Sandwich to marry a widow, Mrs. Rebecca Parker, on June 17, 1773. This union welcomed John Parker Whitewell, a son, baptized on April 3, 1774, and a daughter, Mehetabal, baptized on October 29, 1775. A busy household but a busier community placed its demands upon this pastor of the First Church.

As for the parishioners of the First Church, the names of the streets of Marblehead as well as the history books and the church directory list: Maverick, Stacey, Dixey, Pitman, Gatchell, Pedrick, Reed, Gale, Conant, Legg, Russell, Merritt, Blackler, Dolliber, Darby, Beal, Ward, Bartoll, and Roads. When Thomas Gerry first came to these shores, he was a member, though the rest of his family would join St. Michael's Episcopal Church when it was established. Among names which are synonymous with the Revolution are: Jeremiah Lee, who was married to Martha Swett in the First Church in 1743; Azor Orne; Major Pedrick; Jonathan Glover, though his brother John was a member of the Second Congregational Church; and so on down the list. Rev. Dr. William Bentley, the Salem diarist, was to write in 1804, "These three men [the Glover brothers and Azor Orne] gave a character to Marblehead in the last generation. . . . The leading men [in Marblehead] had power nowhere else known in New England."

Marblehead's population was increasing in the 1760s, and with its expansion of people and escalating business acumen, acute awareness of what was happening in the colonies, in Marblehead in particular, was on the uptrend. The town meeting, which was once called the "megaphone of public sentiment," kept all abreast of every pertinent detail of each happening and vote, and the voters' pulse was heeded. Many dynamic factors were being woven with the threads of the tapestry's scene which would forever portray the Revolution. Marblehead was not only one to be recognized as a leading town in the colonies; its status was also enhanced by its physical location, a fisted elbow of land jutting out into the Atlantic. Probably Marblehead was the foremost fishing port in the entire thirteen colonies, as well as the foremost in Massachusetts in this decade before the Revolution. There were 150 vessels in its fishing fleet, their sizes ranging from 30 to 70 tons, manned by 700 to 800 seamen. Each vessel cost about £450, and its average catch during an eight-month period was nearly 100,000 pounds.

Sixty Marblehead merchants were engaged in foreign commerce, and these merchants were doing well and owned fine homes and slaves. The townspeople became almost as famous for their large families as for their fishing prowess. In 1765 there were just a few short of 5,000 inhabitants, making it the sixth-largest town in the thirteen colonies — behind Newport but ahead of Salem, Baltimore, and Albany. In 1770 the town was second only to Boston in population, wealth, and economic importance in

Massachusetts. George A. Billias wrote *General John Glover and His Marblehead Mariners* in 1860 in which he said,

> Politically Marbleheaders were second only to their Boston neighbors in support of the Revolutionary cause. When changes in imperial policy such as the Sugar Act, and the Townshend Acts placed Boston in the vanguard of the radical movement, Marblehead was only one step behind.

Marblehead's place in history has not had the prominence it deserves; it served the colonies well and vigorously proclaimed and defended its concept of liberty for the entire world to see. The events of the Revolution have been chronicled many times over. Following is a kaleidoscopic view of the role the First Church and its Congregationalists played. (For a list of the men in Glover's Regiment, consult the Appendix of the second edition of Samuel Roads's *History and Traditions of Marblehead*.) Of the 584 men who were in the regiment all but 8 of them were from Marblehead. King George III realized that although the French and Indian War was over there was a great need for more money. Thus, the British Parliament passed the Declaratory Act that could bind the colonists "in all cases whatsoever." The first of Parliament's offenses was the Sugar Act of 1764, for raising revenues on, of course, "sugar, Madeira wine etc." — goods that were carried by Marblehead vessels. The Stamp Act of 1765 would place a high fee on many items, even marriage certificates. It propelled about thirty Marblehead couples to rush into marriage before the act went into effect; many of the First Church's recorded marriages were of that period, but the real hiatus was in the records of the Second Congregational Church. Although the act was repealed the following year, the sting remained acute.

The spirit of patriotism for "the new land" and "the colonies" was mounting. Jeremiah Lee was made the commander of the new "army" of men in Marblehead. Rev. John Barnard reported in 1766 that the troops were

> vigorous and active men so well trained in the use of their arms, and the various motions and marches, that I have heard some Colonels of other regiments and a Brigadier General say they never saw throughout the country ... so goodly an appearance of spirited men, and so well exercised a regiment.

To pursue Marblehead's militia, earlier in October 1774 it was reported that Marbleheaders were turning out "three or four times a week, when Colonel Lee as well as the clergymen [Mr. Whitwell among them] there are not ashamed to appear in the ranks, to be taught the manual exercise

The Old Meeting House on Franklin Street as it was in 1764. The sketch is a side view toward Washington Street.

in particular." The boisterous Revolutionary preparations in Marblehead by the beginning of 1775 had reached such a pitch that they caused Rivington's Tory *New York Gazette* to comment, "The mad-men of Marblehead are preparing for an early campaign against His Majesty's troops."

The "Champagne Charley" Townshend Acts of 1769 duties were leveled on almost every conceivable commodity, which caused radical Boston to head a boycott of British goods. There was at once dissension among the Tories and Whigs of Marblehead, but it proved to be immaterial — a case of taxation without representation was the Greenwich Hospital tax. The Marblehead fishermen (as well as the other colonials) were forced to pay sixpence per voyage to help support the seamans' hospital located in the mother country – a "fur piece" from the Grand Banks that were the fishing grounds for the Marbleheader.

The unproductive Townshend duties, except on tea, went almost unnoticed because of the Boston Massacre on the night of March 5, 1770. A Salem chronicler wrote:

> So enranged are the people of the horrid massacre in Boston ... that no less than Fifteen Hundred men, from this town and Marblehead, would turn out in a minute's warning to revenge the murders, and support the Rights of the insulted and much abused habitants of Boston.

There were a few bright moments for Pastor Whitwell. The church's excellent silver service was added to by Dr. Joseph Lemmon, a Marblehead physician. The outstanding piece of the entire collection was the baptismal bowl designed by Paul Revere and made in his shop. The inscription around the rim reads: "The Donation of Doc. Joseph Lemmon to the First Church of Christ in Marblehead 1773." The bowl also bears the Lemmon coat of arms. According to his will, dated 1772, he left a bequest of "13 pounds, 6 shilling, 8 pence lawfull money" to purchase "a Baptizing Basin."

Also in 1773 Mr. Whitwell would have trying moments, for an epidemic of smallpox broke out in town and the ensuing "smallpox war" had people angry and afraid. John Glover proposed that if Marblehead failed to build a public institution, his group of political leaders would build a private hospital; the sponsors were Jonathan Glover, Jeremiah Lee, Benjamin Marston, and "King" Hooper. These men purchased Cat Island and set up a hospital. Dr. Hall Jackson of Portsmouth, New Hampshire, was well trained for that period, but the inoculation method was not well understood. Townspeople, bound by fear and superstition and the knowledge that their fellow citizens were dying (as well as some being cured), became a mob and forced the closing of the hospital. Thus, reaching the end of their patience, and really fearing for their own safety, Jonathan Glover and his partners capitulated.

In Boston the famous Tea Party had resulted in 90,000 pounds of tea being dumped into the bay. One of the "Indian chiefs" was Dr. Elisha Story of Marblehead! Leading up to the Tea Party the Boston Committee of Grievance issued a circular inviting all neighboring towns to hold meetings "to make a united and successful resistance to this last, worst and most

Painting by an unknown artist of the *Hannah*, the first command in the U.S. Navy, which was built and manned by Marbleheaders and outfitted in Beverly.

destructive measure of administration." Responding, the Marbleheaders assembled at the town house on Tuesday, December 7, 1773, and the meeting was opened with a prayer by the Reverend William Whitwell. Deacon Stephen Phillips was the moderator — "the town desired to be free of the company" (East India Tea Company). Then followed the Boston Tea Party — December 16, 1773.

So many events were demanding serious attention that at the town meeting of May 23, 1774, for which Deacon Stephen Phillips was moderator, a Committee of Correspondence was elected: Joshua Orne, Deacon William Dolliber, Deacon Stephen Phillips, Edward Fettyplace, Capt. John Nutt, and Ebenezer Foster. The meeting was opened with a prayer by the Reverend William Whitwell, whose participation was duly thanked and recorded in the minutes of that day.

The year 1775 was an unforgettable one for all Marbleheaders and for all lovers of freedom and liberty. Camping on Marblehead Neck were British soldiers, and sailing the waters off the North Shore and into the harbor itself were British vessels. One of these, the *Lively* sailed into the harbor on Sunday afternoon, February 26, while the long church service was in progress, and anchored off Homan's Beach. A regiment of British soldiers armed with muskets, under Col. Leslie's command, landed on the beach to start their march to Salem to seize suspected arms secreted here.

Maj. John Pedrick, who was attending the church service, heard the measured beat of the alarm warning of approaching danger drummed on the church door, hastened from the quiet church service, and galloped on horseback along the Dungeons road to warn Salem of Leslie's approach. Fortunately, as he caught up to the advancing regiment which occupied the entire width of the road, he was recognized by the officer in charge (his daughter's suitor) who ordered "file right" (go into single file) to cause no delay in his haste to visit a sick friend. In the meantime, the Marblehead militia was hurrying itself into action. The North River drawbridge was raised to prevent the British from advancing and Leslie's forces were caught between the aroused Salemites and the advancing Marbleheaders. Finding himself in this predicament, Leslie negotiated a face-saving settlement, the bridge was lowered, and he was allowed to march a short distance into Salem and then return to Marblehead and to his vessel.

By April the Marbleheaders were off the "Ye banks" fishing, determined to carry on business until the Fisheries Act took effect (the hated Restraining Act). However, three of the town politicians, Elbridge Gerry, Azor Orne, and Jeremiah Lee, were meeting secretly with Samuel Adams and John Hancock at Weatherby's Black Horse Tavern in Menotomy (now Arlington) on April 18. Being warned of the British soldiers' approach, they hid in the damp fields behind the tavern that day — April 19 — when the "shot heard 'round the world" was fired. From that exposure Jeremiah Lee contracted pneumonia from which he died, leaving a saddened town and his position as leader of the Marblehead militia to John Glover.

Great pressgangs prowled about the streets of the town trying to impress men into the Royal Navy. Many families were pushed beyond endurance, and an exodus to places not so dangerously exposed as Marblehead was begun. One Capt. Thomas Barker arrived from fishing around the middle of May 1775 and enlisted in Capt. Samuel R. Trevett's company of artillery. That same company marched to the old meeting house on May 21 where the Reverend Mr. Whitwell preached a sermon for them. A few days afterward the artillery marched to Cambridge, Massachusetts. The day after the frigate *Lively* sailed for Boston, her place was taken by the sloop *Merlin*. From this moment on Mr. Whitwell's hands were full, for it was his sad duty to move among the homes of his parishioners to cheer and console as news of their sons and husbands who fell on the battlefield or on shipboard in defense of their country reached Marblehead. Trevett's company saw duty at the Battle of Bunker Hill.

In August 1775 John Glover leased to the army his own schooner, the *Hannah,* and manned her with Marblehead seamen — "the first armed vessel fitted out in the service of the United States." Nicholson Broughton, another Marbleheader, was her captain. While the *Hannah* was the first vessel so commanded, she really did little to distinguish herself except be the first named vessel!

In mid-December, John Glover and his Marblehead Regiment joined Gen. George Washington in Cambridge, Massachusetts. They brought with them an awareness of the moments of high danger, the habit of obedience that can mean the difference between life and death — the lesson that life at sea teaches so dramatically. They were not afraid to take orders, and they felt no effrontery in saluting and obeying; more than that, they had a deep grievance against the mother country, for she wished to deprive them of their livelihood — the catching of the cod. They were healthy men and were nattily dressed in cocked hats, abbreviated blue jackets, and loose white trousers. Their adaptability to elements and to situations made them key figures in the days and battles ahead, whether at Dorchester Heights, the East River, New York, or at Pell's Point and Pelham Bay: the storms and the enemy they held off, inflicting many casualties. By 1777 John Glover and his men were known throughout the colonies, as the Battle of Saratoga proved to be a turning point; at Trenton, Glover and his men had ferried some 950 soldiers across the Delaware River to insure the vic-

Gravestone of William Whitwell
on Old Burial Hill.

tory. The valiant fishermen manned oars of Durham boats — flat-bottomed, bargelike craft for transporting ore — carrying the eighteen cannon — a far cry from sailing vessels. The men were ferried in both these and rowboats, and so cold was the weather that by the time the Jersey shore was gained two soldiers were dead, frozen where they sat. Surrender at Yorktown in 1781 ended hostilities.

The war years had been hard on Marblehead; few seaports had endured as much. Her men had enlisted in droves in the military service or had engaged in privateering, and there were 378 widows and 672 fatherless children at the close of the war. The 12,000 tons of shipping owned or manned by Marbleheaders before the war had dwindled to 1,500 tons. With the tenacity that they were noted for, the Marbleheaders made a fine comeback during the 1780s. During this trying period two terrific storms of tremendous force took their toll of men. Nathan Bowen, the chronicler of that time, noted "the tribulations of nature — 'meadow worms' and other pests of agriculture — also tempests and vagaries of weather."

A note from Ashley Bowen's *Day Book* records the generosity of the natives: although Marblehead was recovering from the effects of the smallpox epidemic and had a poor fishing season, the community nevertheless sent 224 quintals of good eating fish to feed Boston's poor. Elbridge Gerry was in charge of the relief program.

In 1767 the Marblehead annual budget was appropriated to include an amount for public education, and trustees were appointed to oversee its use. In April 1781 Joshua Orne, William R. Lee, the Reverend William Whitwell, the Reverend Isaac Story, and Samuel Sewall were elected trustees of the public schools. Here was another facet of Mr. Whitwell's life. At the age of forty-five on November 8, 1781, the minister died. From his first sermon (May 24, 1761) until his demise he had endeared himself to his parishioners and townspeople alike. In his twenty years of ministry he had proved Barnard's faith and expectation of him — he had served God and Marblehead well.

For the next seventeen years (1783-1800) the period of recovery from the pains and privations of the war, the Reverend Ebenezer Hubbard led the church as the town's economy improved and the new country adopted its Constitution. Visits by the Marquis de Lafayette (1784), President George Washington (1789), and Vice President John Adams (1790) supplied much needed inspiration and encouragement to the town's revival and its entry into the nineteenth century.

6

Samuel Dana
Starts the Sunday School

THE 1801-37 PASTORATE of the Reverend Samuel Dana, the third longest and surpassed only by those of Cheever and Barnard, was far more than just the typical long service of a New England Congregational pastor of the early nineteenth century. It was dedicated service to this church during one of the most interesting, moving, and sometimes violent thirty-six years of our country's history.

We must realize that in 1801 the United States was only thirteen years old and consisted of the thirteen original states plus Vermont, Kentucky, and Tennessee. During Dana's pastorate Ohio, Louisiana, Indiana, Mississippi, Illinois, Alabama, Maine, Missouri, Arkansas, and Michigan were added.

John Adams, our second president and a Massachusetts resident, turned over the reins to Thomas Jefferson in 1801. This seemed ominous to many at that time. Political figures were not as oriented to parties as they were to geographical groupings. There were the commercial, industrial Northeast with its owner-operated factories, farms, or boats; the South with its agricultural system based largely upon large plantations and, yes, slavery; and the fast-developing frontier, whose settlements had elements of both of the above, but perhaps a bit more from a freedom-loving New England, and hence leading eventually to the Civil War. After John Adams the only New Englanders in the nation's capital with real political influence

Old North in 1860.

were our Elbridge Gerry, who was vice-president from 1813 to 1817, and John Quincy Adams, who became president in 1825.

This was also a most challenging period for the New England Congregational churches. The Unitarian controversy, the abolitionist movement, the desire for an association of the churches, the need for home and foreign missions and a program for the education of the youth, under the direction of the church, were of paramount importance, and Dr. Dana met the challenge.

Politically, Marblehead and its church enjoyed a few happy years, but then England and its Napoleonic rival started to make life miserable. England was throttling France by the use of its greatest weapon, seapower. Napoleon, although conqueror of a continent, was nevertheless a prisoner in Europe. While the giants, England and France, struggled for domination of Europe and the world, smaller nations such as the United States suffered grievously. American ships and cargoes were confiscated, her trade ruined, and her seamen impressed by both sides. The specter of war darkened America until our government, in a desperate attempt to keep us from being involved in the bitter war between England and the French Empire, placed an embargo on all foreign commerce in 1808. No American ship could sail to foreign ports or even fish well offshore.

In Marblehead (and Salem) there was utter stagnation of commerce; the impoverishment of fishermen, sailors, and workmen; and the ruin of mercantile concerns. Ships rotted at the wharves, and men's souls rusted out in idleness. Maritime Marblehead was kept safe from the perils of war, but the seacoast people were bitter at a government which impoverished them while shielding them from danger. In Parson Dana's church there were men who would rather face the hazards of fishing or trading in waters where the French and British were fighting than to stay home in safety, there to hoe potatoes and dig clams. To these men the sea was life, and land was either a place from which a boat might sail or a haven for those too old to sail. These conditions existed until 1814, when Marbleheaders could sail again.

As an aside, in June 1808 the Reverend Dr. William Bentley, a pastor and historian of Salem, said the embargo had done one good thing: it had greatly encouraged pleasure boating. But it only looked like pleasure boating — it was the restless activity of men bottled up by Jefferson's embargo. Perhaps they needed to fish to put some food on the table! A small gunboat of the U.S. Navy out of Salem patrolled the waters from Winthrop to Cape Ann, but in those days one could catch cod (and even haddock) inside Halfway Rock.

Snow *America* of Marblehead on January 2, 1803, after a water color by M. Corne.

With the inauguration of President James Monroe in 1817 the so-called Era of Good Feeling began and continued until the late 1820s. But this was political good feeling, certainly not small-town New England feeling. The theological disturbance, or Unitarian controversy, promoted great bitterness and sharp contention.

The Unitarians and Universalists were making marked gains, and the old Puritan Congregationalists felt the need of a strong front against what was considered the enemy of pure Christianity. In many towns the affiliation of their parish with Unitarianism left a sizable minority both pastorless and homeless. This was not true in Marblehead. We had two Congregational churches—our First Church and the Second Church. When the Reverend John Bartlett influenced his church to embrace Unitarianism in 1820, our pastor, Samuel Dana, who with his church stood firm in his faith, had been working for several years to insure the continuation of the old faith of our Pilgrim and Puritan fathers. He had established our Sunday school in 1817; he was one of the early proposers of an association of churches and the first moderator of the Essex South Association of Churches; and he was a supporter of home and foreign missions. There was even an Essex County missionary (Francis Danforth of Andover Theological Seminary) and later others "to be employed among the waste places" of Essex County.

Ship *Mary*, built in Marblehead in 1854, as painted by Wm. York in 1879.

In 1716 a ministers association was formed for Essex County Congregational ministers, but not until May 8, 1827, was there one for churches with both lay and clerical delegates. On that day the ministers and delegates of Congregational churches from Lynn to Rockport gathered in Marblehead's "new stone meetinghouse" and formed the Essex South Conference of Churches, now known as the Essex South Association of the United Church of Christ. The Reverend Samuel Dana, chosen moderator, had on that day been twenty-seven years in the pastorate of the Marblehead church.

A still more marked force than the disorganization of work through theological difference was the desire that the full strength of the churches be brought to bear in the service of the Lord: namely, the great missionary movement which had its birth in the first years of the new century. The American Board of Commissioners for Foreign Missions was founded in 1810, and on May 12, 1826, the American Home Missionary Society was formed. A united group of Congregational churches was needed to support these endeavors. Under Samuel Dana the First Church of Marblehead supported these benevolent activities, as it has to this day.

Now we come to one of the most outstanding stars in Parson Dana's crown — the establishment of the Sunday school. The first session was held on Sunday, May 18, 1817, at eight o'clock in the morning with the

Reverend Mr. Dana as its first superintendent, in the old Franklin Street meetinghouse (built in 1695 to replace the one on Old Burial Hill). It was located across the street from the present Franklin Street fire station and Rev. John Barnard's old parsonage. With it high-backed box pews, it was far from ideal for classes, so a chapel was built on Pearl Street the very next year. Perhaps the distance from the church to the chapel was one of the factors in the relocation of the church to the new stone meetinghouse which this parish built in 1824 and in which we worship today. Of course, the principal factors were the age of the old Franklin Street meetinghouse and the desire to get away from the continual repair of an old wooden building.

This school was intended for children who received little or no religious instruction at home. They were taught passages of Scripture, hymns, and the catechism. To those who could not read, the stories of the bible were told until they knew them by heart. This school was continued until November and then closed for the winter, since there was no heating system.

Church records and town records were kept with great accuracy in the early years of the colony and later statehood. All town meetings were held in our church until the erection of the "old town house" in 1727. But this recordkeeping did not carry over into the Sunday school. We have no evidence that a record of the first year of the school was kept. But in 1884 Nathan P. Sanborn wrote:

Thirty years ago there were many, and there are now a few persons living, who well remember that first Sunday School. The old-fashioned high square pews hid from view the classes scattered about the church, and as one entered after the opening of the session, no person was seen, but the hum of suppressed voices was heard from every part of the house; and occasionally the sharp creaking of a revolving baluster, put in motion by some little thoughtless or mischievous restless hand that had become weary of the restraints of the hour; some of the occupants of those pews, having recited their lessons, had listened to the ticking of the clock that hung against the front of the singers' gallery; had estimated the probabilities of a catastrophe by the falling of the sounding-board, and counted the golden stars that were above the pulpit, wondering if they had been captured from the sky, or made to order; now wished to settle the question, whether any of the little balusters that surrounded the tops of the pews, could be revolved to the right with less noise than if revolved to the left.

We also have no record of who were the teachers serving under the Reverend Mr. Dana's superintendency, but we do have a record of the teaching staff one year later, in 1818. Under Nathan Bowen as superintendent there were fourteen men teaching boys and nineteen ladies teaching girls. The session was to continue "not less than one hour and a quarter or more than two hours, at any season of the year." No child was to be admitted under five years of age, and no one allowed to read in the school who could not read without spelling; and "if any not thus qualified shall attend, other means for their instruction shall be provided."

It is reasonable to assume that many of those teaching in 1818 were carryovers from the original staff, and it appears that Mr. Bowen was a teacher that first year. For those who might like to spot the name of one of their old Marblehead ancestors, the following teachers were added in 1819: John Russell, John Lecraw, Ichabod Phillips, Michael Doak, George Trask, Rebecca Kimball, Sally Dennis, Sally W. Bray, Hannah Lovitt, and Hannah Homan.

In 1820 the school opened on the first Sunday in May with Joseph Merrill as superintendent and eleven male and twelve female teachers. The following names appear for the first time on the list of teachers: Samuel Putnam, Elisha Huntington, Margaret Grant, Phillippa Call, and Charlotte Lewis.

In 1821 the school opened again on the first Sunday in May with Richard Homan as superintendent, and this gentleman was annually reelected to that office until his death on October 16, 1851. It is interesting to note that Mr. Homan and many of our church school superintendents served also as deacons of the church.

While it is often possible to find who was baptized or joined the church in the 1600s, it is nearly impossible to get any factual data on Sunday school membership or activities in the early 1800s! But we do have a record of our school superintendents; those who served during the years covered by this chapter were:

Rev. Samuel Dana	1817-1818
Nathan Bowen	1818-1820
Joseph Merrill	1820-1821
Richard Homan	1821-1851

Aside from the founder, the Reverend Samuel Dana, several of the early workers in our school seem to have been almost legendary characters of Marblehead. William Reed, who withdrew from the Second Church when its leanings became Unitarian and became a member of our church, was active in the early Sunday school movement in Marblehead and in Massachusetts in general as well. This promoter of Christian education was the principal contributor toward the erection of the new stone meetinghouse in which we worship today. His picture hangs in the church parlor. Richard Homan served as superintendent for thirty years, and Nathan P. Sanborn (from whose records much of this was written) served in that position for thirty-four years!

If one of those who was present during that first year of 1817 were present today, would he recognize anything? Although the building we worship in today was not built until 1824, seven years later some relics of both the first and second meetinghouses are in use today. The old silver communion service, Paul Revere baptismal bowl, box pew ends now at the southwest corner of the sanctuary, and the codfish weather vane are a few. He would see the same pulpit, although not now mounted on an hour-glass base with a sounding board above it. The old pulpit Bible going back to Parson Barnard's day, and perhaps the Bible dated 1817 which was in the parlor bookcase, were used in that historic year.

Ecumenicity came early to Marblehead, for on May 22, 1818, several prominent citizens of the town, noting the success of our church school, met at the "new meetinghouse," which was the Second Congregational Church on what is now Mugford Street, and measures were taken for the organization of a Sabbath School Union Society. At a subsequent meeting held at Academy Hall on Pleasant Street, a constitution was adopted, and the society was organized. The Honorable William Reed was elected president.

It is very difficult to get accurate records of what happened that day in 1818, but it is believed that representatives of our First Church (Rev. Samuel Dana), the Second Church (Rev. John Bartlett), the Baptist Church (gathered in 1810), St. Stephen's Methodist Church, and St. Michael's Episcopal Church decided to conduct cooperative church schools similar to, and in conjunction with, the one organized at the First Church. After a very few years denominational interests caused the dissolution of the Marblehead Sabbath School Union Society, and each church went its own way. The Honorable William Reed, who had transferred his membership to our First Church, later served as president of the Sabbath School Union of Massachusetts, It is sad to note that this gentleman died in Academy Hall on February 17, 1837, while preparing for a celebration by the Sunday school of our church.

When Samuel Dana began his long pastorate, the Franklin Street meetinghouse was in sad shape. It was a 106-year-old wooden building. Paint or stain was seldom used; weathered wood was the norm for one's house, and the same was true for the Lord's house. The church building was not just a church; it was also a place of assembly for the town. Repair and maintenance were the responsibility of the selectmen and the town meeting. Sparse as these were, they became even less when the old town house was built and occupied in 1727. This was a time, peculiar to New England Congregationalism, when there was a distinct dual responsibility for the building and its use. There was The Society (sometimes parish) and The Church — the former for providing and maintaining a building, pews, a tower, and a bell; the latter for settling a minister, filling the pews, and ringing the bell. A vestige of this organization still exists with the responsibilities of the trustees versus those of the church committee. When the town meeting moved to the new town house, the old meetinghouse became the complete responsibility of the church people, although it was occasionally used for highly attended town meetings.

The hopes of building and moving to a new stone meetinghouse were dim during Dana's first lean years. But with what one could call a revival (perhaps started by the success and needs of the Sunday school) and which resulted in increased interest, support, membership, and desire, the goal seemed possible. By 1821 it could be attainable because one of the new members, the Honorable William Reed, agreed to provide the major part of the cost. A lot of land was purchased, and the stately building with its beautiful tower was built in 1824. It is where we worship today.

When dedicated in 1825 it did not have a granite front, just the rough brown ashlar wall which is present today on the back and sides. The interior was very plain — "bare as a meetinghouse wall" would certainly apply. There was no organ; an old bass viol was used until 1834. In January

Portrait of William Reed by an unknown artist now hangs in the parlor of Old North.

1826 the church voted to put a stove in the pulpit! It felt the need to warm its minister, if not its congregation. The first furnace was put into the church in December 1826, but this served only to keep listening ears from freezing, and it was not until 1841 that adequate heating was furnished for the congregation.

Parson Dana, at his death, left this church and Marblehead with many accomplishments to his credit. The old decayed wooden meetinghouse had been replaced by a handsome stone church; a church school had been established which continues to this day; membership and enthusiasm had greatly increased; and a strong church was on its way into the next period of our country's history, which was destined to be so turbulent.

7

The Turbulent Years

A S ONE SURVEYS the period from 1835 to 1885, it is difficult to imagine how so many momentous occurrences could be concentrated in such a relatively small span of time. The world experienced the Second French Revolution of 1848, the Industrial Revolution and the problems it created, Charles Darwin's theories, Karl Marx's propaganda, and a worldwide zeal for missionary and religious activity. The United States, in addition to being affected by events of the rest of the world, experienced a tremendous westward expansion; the Indian wars; a rush of states joining the Union; a war with Mexico; and the continuing, escalating argument between slavery and abolition which resulted in the Civil War. The happenings in and around Marblehead and Old North Church were not so grand as those in the nation and around the world, but Marbleheaders became involved as they always do, and national events left their marks here as well as on other places in our country.

It might be of benefit to look at this period in three time segments to well understand the progression of events that carried the world and the nation along at near breakneck speed. Let us deal first with the period from 1835 to approximately 1855, when events began to create sharp divisions between the North and the South.

Any important happenings in the world, regardless of how regionalized they seem, will generally later influence some distant spot, and so it was with several events which occurred immediately before the beginning of our time period. During the years 1831-32 Jamaica experienced a bloody

Old North in the mid-1800s, from an early stereograph.

slave uprising which resulted in the slaves' emancipation in 1834. After years of national discord, all slaves within the British Empire were emancipated in 1833. In the same year, the first effective Factory Act — to deal with "white slaves" and children in factories — was passed in England. Society was beginning to address some of the ills that had been created by the Industrial Revolution. The Industrial Revolution, quite simply, was a case of increasing populations creating expanding markets, and manufacturers were driven to employ technical innovations to make up for a scarcity of appropriate labor. The major breakthrough, an improved form of the steam engine, gave manufacturers a source of power independent of climate and season and did not limit them with regard to geographic location, thus (among other factors) producing an urban society.

Churches in England at the time were dominated by the concept of class, so most of the urban masses had no one to tend to their spiritual needs. It was not until the 1840s that the Church of England was able to respond. By this time people had been questioning the effects that industrialization was having on their lives and the lives of others. A great wave of social and religious reform was sweeping over Europe. Hymn singing in church became acceptable within the Church of England several years before; as a result, a profusion of hymnbooks were written, and music in churches rose in popularity.

With so much trouble on their own continent, it is not surprising that the European nations left the United States alone during this period, but Americans were not sitting idly by; indeed, the pace of events was equally hectic in America.

The United States was expanding in several ways at once — by the admission of new states, land acquisitions, westward expansion, and the infusion of hordes of immigrants. Social and religious reforms proliferated in the turmoil of these times.

Congregationalists founded the American Missionary Association in 1846. It carried on some work among Eskimos and Indians, but primarily it led the way in the establishment of schools for blacks in the South. Atlanta, Howard, Fisk, Talladega, Willard, Tougaloo, and Tillotson colleges and universities are examples of the work of this association. Congregationalists emphasized the meaning and value of the individual under God without underemphasizing the meaning and value of human society. A national consciousness was developing as representatives of the many Congregational churches were called together in 1846 and again in 1852 to consider matters of national interest in the denomination.

Much was also happening in Marblehead during this busy period from 1835 to 1855. Just prior to this period the Unitarian movement had swept over the Congregational churches of Massachusetts and had a great deal of momentum by the time it reached Marblehead. Although the first churches of Plymouth, Cambridge, Salem, and other towns, plus all the churches of Boston founded before 1700 with the exception of the Old South Congregational had became Unitarian, Rev. Samuel Dana held the First Church (Old North Church) to its course. When the pastor of the Second Church went over to Unitarianism, many left that church and gathered about Mr. Dana. Notable among these was the Honorable William Reed.

After a ministry of thirty-six years in Marblehead, the Reverend Mr. Dana and his associate for the last five years, the Reverend Samuel Cozzens, resigned and on April 18, 1837, the traditional Council of Dismissal accepted the resignations. In August of that year Reverend Mark A. H. Niles was installed as pastor. (It should be noted that the resignations were not related to the question of Unitarianism nor were they dismissed in the sense that they were discharged.)

Interior of Lyon's shoe shop on Front and Circle Streets, which still stands today.

In these years Marblehead was rapidly changing from a fishing town with some small businesses into a town primarily engaged in manufacturing, but it maintained a large fishing fleet at the same time. The shoe business was beginning to centralize, replacing the "ten-footers," the small shops where fishermen made heavy boots between trips and during the winter. Other small manufacturing businesses were emerging, such as cordage, wheels, furniture, candles, soaps, and glue. In fact, the total worth of manufactured goods was more than double the worth of the fishermen's business, despite the fact that the fleet consisted of ninety-five vessels, each over fifty tons. Marblehead, with its 5,500 people, was virtually a boom town.

The Reed Fund was probated in May 1837, providing help to the poor or needy in our parish. (The Reed Fund is still in use in our church today.) The church appeared to hold a tight rein on the attitudes and behavior of its members. From the church records: "Margaret Sullivan restored to church membership after having shown penitence for breaking the 7th Commandment"; "Brother Manning was called before the deacons of the church for drunkedness — was penitent and signed the pledge"; and in 1847 several members were questioned and admonished

Pages from the church records of 1854.

for frequenting the bowling alley.

Rev. Edward A. Lawrence became the pastor of Old North in 1845, after Rev. Niles's resignation in 1844, and guided the church until 1854 when he accepted a professorship of church history and pastoral duty in the East Windsor Theological Seminary. During his pastorate Marblehead faced many trials and challenges. In 1846 the town suffered the worst devastation to its fishing fleet ever recorded. Sixty-five men and boys were lost in a storm which left 43 widows and 155 fatherless children.

Yet, business optimism remained high in the town, and changes were continual. The first townwide official fire department was formed consisting of five wards with men allotted to each district. By 1848 plans were in progress for a direct railroad to Boston, and the following year 3,700 tons of freight were hauled from Marblehead to Boston.

But, despite the changes, despite the optimism, the question of slavery was on mens' minds. Harriet Beecher Stowe's *Uncle Tom's Cabin* (1852) fanned the flames of conscience. The building currently housing our church offices played a unique part in the abolition cause. The structure is probably three centuries old, and it housed Marblehead's staunchest abolitionists, Samuel and Thomas M. Goodwin. From 1841 until President Lin-

The Third Congregational (South) Church.

coln's Emancipation Proclamation, these brothers were untiring in their efforts on behalf of the slaves in the South. At this early period the abolitionist cause was not universally popular, and the Goodwins were often ridiculed and their efforts bitterly opposed by their neighbors. In addition to bringing abolitionist speakers to the town, they were also active members of the Underground Railroad, sheltering fugitive slaves and assisting them on their road to Canada and freedom. The Stacey House was used to conceal the slaves until they could be safely forwarded to the next station. With its many stairs, hallways, and concealed areas, the Stacey House was ideally suited for this purpose. It must be remembered that such activity was a crime, since slaves were legal possessions of their masters. The Goodwins must have acted out of a deep feeling of conscience, because the consquences of their actions could have been most unpleasant.

This segment closes with the installation of Rev. Benjamin R. Allen as pastor in November 1854. His pastorate covered the entire period of the Civil War.

The second segment of our fifty-year period covers the years from 1855 to 1870, including the years leading up to the Civil War, the Civil War years themselves, and the several years following the war. The world was awed by the explorations of David Livingstone, shocked by the evolution theories of Charles Darwin, and angered by the political writings of Karl Marx. Nationally, the events leading up to the Civil War overshadowed everything else that was happening, and so much information is available on the war that it serves little purpose for us to go into any additional detail. All institutions seemed to be affected by the issues and the war. Churches óf both the North and the South used the bible to attack or defend slavery, depending on the interpreters' sentiments, with the result that many churches split, never to reach reconciliation when the war ended. This segment was also a busy one in Marblehead. In 1858 the South Church (more properly, the Third Church) was built, causing the First Church to be "renamed" Old North. The formation of the South Church was evidently the result of a controversy that arose within the congregation, and forty members withdrew to form the new church. It was not long afterward, in April 1861, that newly elected President Lincoln found it necessary to call on the northern states to raise troops for the Union cause. Marblehead responded immediately, with the Marblehead Sutton Light Infantry, the Lafayette Guards, and the Glover Light Guards being mustered in Boston the day following the call. They paraded through Marblehead and in Boston to Faneuil Hall with much fanfare, for most northerners were of the opinion that a few months' duty and the show of Union force would be all that was needed to settle the whole affair. They were dreadfully wrong in their assessment of the situation.

Many of those who went off to serve left families who were dependent on them. This need was met as the town set up a relief fund, schoolteachers voted to contribute 6 percent of their salaries, and the women of the town set up a benefit committee. Mary Graves was president and Mary Alley was secretary of this benefit committee. The women also donated time and materials to fashion uniforms for volunteers.

At the beginning of the war there were no standard uniforms for either army. Each unit that was raised had its own uniform, many gaudy beyond belief. This lack of standard uniforms for troops presented some confusion at the First Battle of Bull Run where some Union forces had gray uniforms and some Confederates had blue. Two months after the first units were called, another company, the Mugford Guards, was raised and sent off to support the northern cause.

By the summer of 1862 the war efforts in the West and in Virginia had indelibly etched names such as Manassas Junction, Shiloh, Corinth, and Vicksburg in the minds of people of the North, and the long casualty lists and the sorrow of personal losses had replaced the excitement and adventure of going off to fight a war. It is not surprising that recruitments had fallen off drastically. Special efforts were made to procure recruits including the payment of a $100 bounty to each man who would volunteer for three years. There was also concern that the Confederate warships might attack northern ports, so Fort Sewall, which was virtually in ruins, was rebuilt, armed, and garrisoned. Finally a draft was instituted, creating riots in New York and Boston. One hundred and eighty Marbleheaders were selected in the local draft at Lyceum Hall in Salem, but many were able to pay a commutation fee of $300 or purchase a substitute to take their place.

The long tradition of Marbleheaders in the navy continued in the Civil War. The combined total of servicemen from Marblehead was 1,048, a surplus of 91 over its quota and nearly 14 percent of the total population of the town. Marbleheaders fought valiantly, and many local homes were affected by the continuing casualties. But finally the war came to a close; and the citizens began to sort out their lives. In 1868 a group was organized to create a memorial to the soldiers and sailors who had lost their lives in the service of their country.

A national gathering of Congregational churches was held in Boston in 1865 to discuss the needs of the South following the Civil War and a variety of other matters. It also approved a statement of faith and a formulation of policy, involving the autonomy of the local church, the fellowship of the churches, and a nonhierarchical ministry.

Locally, Old North was still being led by the Rev. Mr. Allen. He was a man of strong convictions, and during the war his conservatism apparently was not always in harmony with supporters of the administration in Washington. Despite the fact that his political views sometimes differed from those of other Marblehead and Old North people, he was always respected, and he gave the impression that he was acting from a profound sense of duty.

The church had for some time felt the need for a parsonage. In 1868 a site on High Street was purchased with a wide view of land and sea. To finance this purchase, some land belonging to the church was sold; a total of $1,800 in donations was received; and the Ladies' Parish Society, long an important factor in the history of the church, raised a sum of $2,200. Mr. Allen had the pleasure of moving into the parsonage in late 1869.

As we enter the last segment of our period, 1870-85, we see that world and national events were continuing at the same hurried pace. The Vatican had, by now, lost all its political power, and the pope had moved to in-

The old parsonage at 23 High Street with Rev. J. H. Williams by the fence.

crease the spiritual power of his position by proclaiming the dogma of papal infallibility regarding matters of faith and morals. Shortly afterward, but not as a result of this, the Catholic church was deprived of all church lands except Vatican City and several other small properties. Also, Louis Pasteur developed the technique of immunization against disease, General Custer made his famous Last Stand, Mark Twain wrote *The Adventures of Tom Sawyer,* and Thomas Edison invented the incandescent light bulb.

The Congregational churches followed up on their earlier convention by calling together the first National Council at Oberlin in 1871, and a constitution was adopted providing for a meeting every third year. The constitution revealed the characteristic adaptability of Congregationalism. The autonomy of the local church was fully preserved; at the same time, the fellowship of the churches was provided for at three levels: (1) the local association, meeting usually twice a year, often following county lines, to which each Congregational church would send its pastor and delegates; (2) the State Conference, meeting annually, to which churches belonging to the associations would send pastors and delegates; and (3) the General Council, now meeting every two years, to which associations and conferences would send both ministerial and lay delegates. This remains the way our church organization functions today. A sentence from the "Declaration of the Unity of the Church," adopted at this Council, is characteristic of Congregationalism's view of all churches and religions. It states: "As little as did our fathers in their day, do we in ours make a pretension to be the only churches of Christ."

Rev. John H. Williams was installed as Old North's pastor in September 1873, replacing the Reverend Mr. Allen, who had died fifteen months earlier. The Reverend Mr. Williams had graduated from Andover Theological Seminary just prior to his installation.

On the morning of June 25, 1877, there occurred another great tragedy for the town, this being the great fire which consumed the larger part of the business blocks of the town and effectively ended the shoe industry in Marblehead. The meetinghouse of the Third Church was also lost in this conflagration. Old North immediately invited the members of the Third Church to occupy its church or chapel. After a few weeks it was learned that the Third Church would not rebuild, and a cordial invitation was extended for it to unite with Old North. On the first Sunday in September, fifty-five members presented their letters and entered the church.

It had been apparent that the chapel on Pearl Street was too small for the needs of the church. Many persons were reportedly turned away from the Sunday evening prayer meetings for want of room. In the summer of 1878 there was support to purchase land adjoining the church on Washington Street and build a new chapel. In the fall this was put to a vote and was passed. The new building was completed during the winter and was dedicated on March 12, 1879. At its dedication an outstanding debt of $3,300 still remained, which was cause for great concern. But the weekly offering system and the Ladies' Parish Society combined to raise the necessary monies, and the last dollar of the debt was paid off in April 1882, only three years after the dedication.

In January 1883 Rev. John Williams resigned to accept a call from the Clyde Congregational Church of Kansas City, Missouri. He was succeeded by the Reverend S. Linton Bell of Lincolnshire, England, who was installed on February 28, 1884. The Reverend Mr. Bell was described as an able leader, to whom the people were strongly attached.

All periods of history seem filled with change, and our fifty-year period from 1835 to 1885 is certainly no exception. What was different in this period was the incredible magnitude and the dizzying pace of the changes that transpired. In earlier years changes seemed to occur at a steady yet natural pace, but the combination of the Industrial Revolution and the Civil War during this one time period removed the element of naturalness and began to force changes on society. These years were tumultous in every sense, and the new pace simply became the new standard. Marblehead, like most other communities, took up the pace and integrated it with the unique and peculiar aspects of the town. The only certainty was that the changes were irreversible, that a new period, with its new challenges, was dawning.

8

Conscience
and the Modern Times

THE YEAR IS 1880. Imagine, if you will, being an eye in the sky looking down on the planet Earth. The Europeans have taken control of Africa, leaving only Christian Ethiopia and Liberia still struggling to retain their independence. Germany, through the production of coal and iron, has forged ahead as one of the leaders in the great Industrial Revolution which is sweeping the West. Even Asia has succumbed to the fever of mechanical progress, modernizing railways as well as strengthening metal and textile mills.

In India the British have somehow failed to see that the education of the Indian upper classes is resulting in their disenchantment with British rule and supremacy.

In the arts, realism is the cry of the day. French author Emile Zola and English author Thomas Hardy have veered from romantic tales of the well to do and are writing about angry miners and country villagers. Sigmund Freud is revolutionizing the study of psychology. Poet Arthur Rimbaud, dramatist Henrik Ibsen, and satirist Oscar Wilde are looking at bourgeois life and dismissing it as stultifying. New ideas, new isms, and new credos are titillating and sometimes shocking the world.

Society has made the choice to advance with industrialism. The agrarian ideal will from this time on be secondary to material and technological advances. Within this context, religion must stretch to maintain its place of relevance to the dazzled humans caught up in the tide of change.

Let us now look down upon America. The blackened mines of Pennsylvania, the clacking looms of Lowell, the iron beds surrounding the Great Lakes, the whirring saws of Wisconsin and Minnesota, and, yes, the hammering of nails in the shoe shops of Lynn and Marblehead — all bear witness to the fact that America is the cradle of this same revolution. It is apparent, moreover, that the leaders of this great dynamic democracy believe in this wave, believe that America should hold high the shining light of progress by which the rest of the world is to be guided.

Let us go back, then, to examine the relation of the church in general, and of one church in particular, to this world and this society.

The church in America was beginning to recognize that a great question existed in the minds of many of its clergy and members. This question had been posed by clerics and sociologists alike. Could the heart of man be truly redeemed in the midst of often oppressive and sometimes seemingly hopeless conditions? Social problems had begun to seem overwhelming. Could the soul of man be freed from the realities of slums, child labor abuses, and greed in the marketplace?

Many a good person, raised on the venerable New England belief in the Protestant work ethic, was confused and threatened by the strikes, lockouts, boycotts, and riots of the late century. Was it not decent and honorable to make an honest profit and prosper? Could business owners of personal rectitude truly be the devils painted by the more radical labor organizers? To complicate things, certain ministers had begun to speak out on a national level. In the late 1800s, Washington Gladden, a Congregational minister from Columbus, Ohio, and Walter Rauschenbusch, a Baptist pastor, spoke movingly about a society which seemed to care more for profits than for the human and divine rights of man. Gladden supported labor but was equally critical of both labor and capital when they refused to cooperate for the betterment of mankind.

All over America the Christian picked up his paper and read of conditions which bred disease, vice, and crime. Gradually, the great Christian conscience was aroused, and men and women of goodwill in and out of the church began to see the necessity not only to address the ills of society but also to understand how to fit the many contradictions they saw into the context of a Christian life.

In Marblehead the gap between the haves and the have-nots was becoming wider than the harbor. But, what to do about it? Charles Sheldon, in his 1896 book, *In His Steps*, proposed that volunteers from the First Church not do anything without first asking "What would Jesus do?" Indeed, what would Jesus do about the growing chasm between the working people of Marblehead and the wealthy owners of yachts who were

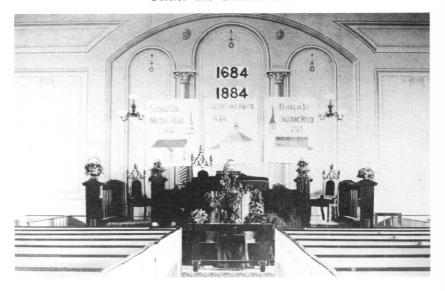

The 200th anniversary, 1884.

beginning to make Marblehead their summer home?

Protestantism must now strive to embrace owner and worker alike under the banner of the Christian law of brotherhood. It must be supposed that there were a few uneasy pew mates in the stone church (the stone meetinghouse) in those days!

Finally, let us look at the First Congregational Church of Marblehead during the score of years before 1900.

The congregation held its services in the stone church on Washington Street. The Reverend John Williams was pastor. Primary matters were decided by the standing committee elect of the First Congregational Society of Marblehead, an imposing title for a dedicated group of men who attended to the financial affairs of the church. The church also held a regular meeting to deal with personal and personnel matters. The records of these meetings make dry reading, but every once in awhile there is something there that piques the interest. In 1881, for example, the church committee recommended that a certain four members be called up before them to "make any statement of resolve, confession, or penitence" for having been "guilty of such neglect of Christian duties and guilty of such Unchristian conduct as demands some action on the part of the church." Whatever had they done? Temperance did not become law in town until 1886, so

Aftermath of the great fire of December 25, 1888.

it must have been misbehavior of a different kind. In any case, two of the four miscreants appeared, properly humbled and sorry, and were "continued in fellowship with the church." Another sinner did not show his face until 1899, at which time he was readmitted and shown the hand of friendship. The other fellow must have just gone on unredeemed! The records are discreet.

People paid for pews then; the better the seat, the higher the price. In 1901 one such half pew sold for $4. The minister's salary in 1880 was $1,500; in 1915 his salary was still $1,500. It would seem that no one cared much about cost-of-living increases back then. Those men of God must have been saintly indeed to live with no raise in thirty-five years! The pastor did, however, get four weeks vacation. It should also be noted that although the women in those days were very generous with their bequests and financial contributions, they were not invited to sit on any committee which had anything to do with the disbursement of such monies.

In 1883 the church membership was 258, the female members outnumbering the male by about four to one. That same year Pastor Williams answered a call to a tiny ministry in Kansas. He left with love and good wishes.

Also in 1883 the church decided to have a celebration of its 200th an-

Washington Street and Old North, 1890.

niversary, which would be in 1884. A committee consisting of Pastor Williams, Nathan P. Sanborn, and James Gregory was formed to celebrate this joyous occasion. (Here we see the women at work, on the entertainment committee!)

In honor of the fete the church was made structurally sound; new furniture was bought; and the old pulpit was banished to the attic, not to reappear for rededication until the 300th celebration in 1935.

When the big day rolled around on August 13, the ceremonies were presided over by the new minister, the Reverend S. Linton Bell ("Lately of England, at present residing in Salem, Mass.") And he remained a citizen of Britain until his death, although the Marbleheaders thought of him as 100 percent American by then. On that happy day the front of the church was decked with flowers; anthems were sung; sermons were given; histories of times and buildings were presented; and finally a confession of faith and a church covenant which had originally been made on August 13, 1684, was read.

The new pastor, S. Linton Bell, has been described as a man of great intellectual force. He was a good man to have around in an age of skepticism and confusion. His sermons are said to have provided a strong ap-

The *Alice* leaves Marblehead harbor for a Corinthian Yacht Club race on July 23, 1891.

proach to modern thinking. He also had a friendly way about him which endeared him to the townspeople. During his ministry the Christian Endeavor group prospered, and the young people of the parish began to speak up.

In 1886 the town went dry. Men's clubs sprang up like dandelions after a spring rain. The yacht clubs were introducing a new lifestyle to Marblehead. Imagine being a fisherman's young son or daughter and watching from across the harbor the pomp and glamor of the Eastern Yacht Club's new opening in 1881. It must have seemed like Cinderella's castle, glimmering across the water. No wonder the old-timers often found the yachting crowd to be a threat to their simple way of life! Many of these same summer people from the Eastern, Boston, and Corinthian yacht clubs came to the First Congregational Church. Boardinghouses and hotels appeared. The character of the town was changing. The church had to absorb these changes and carry on.

In 1886 it was decided that the rough stone or ashlar front of the church needed rebuilding. The generous sum of $5,000 was given by Sarah B. Fettyplace on behalf of the estate of Lucy C. D. Fettyplace. At this time the embankment in front of the church was lowered, and new modern

View from Crocker Park, May 29, 1898.

pews and orchestra seats for the choir were installed. During the renovation of the granite front, a silver plate was discovered behind the stone marked MDCCCXXIV. On this plate was engraved;

THIS TEMPLE

For the worship of Jehovah, Father, Son and Holy Ghost is the First Church in Marblehead, constituted April 13, 1684, was erected A.D. MDCCCXXIV, Samuel Dana, pastor, under the direction of William Reed, Calvin Briggs and Dan Weed, agents of the society principally by the munificence of individuals, and more than all others of

Hon. William Reed

Laus Deo!

This plate and other memorabilia were put into a copper box and rebuilt into the church.

During the presidency of Grover Cleveland, while the West was being won and more states were joining a thriving Union, disaster struck little Marblehead. The terrible Christmas fire of 1888 destroyed the same commercial part of town which had gone up in flames a decade before. This time the shoe factories did not reemerge like the phoenix but died in ashes. Fifty buildings were lost, and 2,000 people were put out of work (this in a town that in 1900 numbered only 7,582 souls!). The Reverend S. Linton

Church interior in the early 1900s.

Bell at Old North and his congregation joined the town in aiding the victims and the unemployed. Once again the gap between the struggling and the affluent seemed vast. The town and the church strove for "honorable cooperation rather than fierce competition." There can be little doubt that the quiet benevolence and progressive spirit of Pastor Bell did much to keep the church in fellowship with the community.

On May 16, 1897, the First Congregational Sunday school celebrated its eightieth birthday under the leadership of Pastor Bell and Superintendent John S. Broughton.

Two services were held. At the morning service Leonard Humphrey recited "Grandpa's Sunshine," a rendition which could hardly have left a dry eye in the house. Etta Dinsmore performed "The Little Preacher," and it is to be hoped that the church membership was sufficiently doting to suffer the little children, as the angels offered up fourteen selections in the morning and at least seventeen in the evening.

Perhaps the spirit of the Sunday school was most eloquently articulated by Nathan P. Sanborn, who served as its superintendent from 1856 until 1889. In his letter of resignation he wrote:

As the tide sets into our bay and goes out again, carrying to the wide ocean the flavor of the shore against which it surges, so since that time more than sixteen hundred have come in and gone out, have joined and left our school, going out into the world with shades of character and impressions different from what they would have been had they never come in with us.

This letter, beautifully composed and obviously the work of a caring and dedicated man, reveals a strong personal awareness of the ways in which good teachings and loving examples can be carried forth from a small group to the farthest reaches on earth. Nathan Sanborn's name appears frequently in the records of this time as treasurer, committeeman, and in many other capacities. Too often the names inscribed in old ink do not show us the man, but this letter brings him up from the past into timeless relevance.

The Sunday school had a long and active run during this era with yet another celebration in 1904 on the occasion of the eighty-seventh anniversary.

Following are a few more statistics which caught the researcher's eye. In 1890 the church spent more money on music ($354.16) than was spent for fuel ($178.82). Can you imagine how delighted our current choir director would be to have those proportions maintained today? On the other side, however, it is noted that a private music school which requested the use of the chapel for a recital was unanimously turned down! One more thing to make you smile, or possibly cry, in light of the fiscal realities of 1984: in 1890 the tax on the parsonage on High Street was $54.94.

The Spanish-American War broke out with the sinking of the *Maine* in 1898. Marblehead sent its boys to fight for its country as it had so often done before. Once again the great moral dilemmas of war were considered by the church. Gold was discovered in the Klondike in that same year. The town lost population between 1900 and 1905.

In 1903 the Reverend Nicholas Van der Pyl, formerly of Holliston, became pastor of the First Church following the much-mourned death from illness of Samuel Linton Bell. The Reverend Dr. Van der Pyl was a magnetic personality, and his ability to interest and inform attracted many good and thoughtful minds. His series of Sunday evening meetings brought in numbers of men from all faiths. On these occasions the chapel overflowed with discourse and interdenominational exchange of ideas. How lively his speech could be is evident in a talk he gave at the 300th anniversary of the church in 1935. At that time he described life in Marblehead and in the church as it had been during the legendary 1890s. He said:

Human nature is very much the same in every age. The innocence and the modesty in the much burlesque gay '90s is only a fiction mainly based upon the long skirts, high-necked dresses, and the tyranny of Mrs. Grundy. We who lived in that period can tell some stories which rival the risqué stories told of Hollywood today.

In 1901 President McKinley was assassinated and was succeeded by Teddy Roosevelt who, in turn, was followed by William Howard Taft. The Progressive movement of the new century was under way.

In 1907 Dr. John Barnett succeeded Nicholas Van der Pyl as pastor and stayed three years. He was described as being handsome and scholarly, and his well-fashioned sermons were considered guides for Christian living. During his ministry the church celebrated its 225th anniversary. A manual was published including a history of the church and a list of members. The trays of the presently used individual communion glasses were purchased to replace the earlier practice of passing the silver heritage cups from person to person throughout the church, and the use of the four flagons for keeping them filled.

In 1910 Dr. Barnett's place was taken by the Reverend Leslie C. Greeley, a graduate of Boston University and Andover Theological Seminary. His positive stands served as a dependable rudder during the times leading up to World War I.

The church had always contributed to worthwhile causes. In 1911 members gave $2,153 to the Anti-Saloon League and $628 to the Women's Christian Temperance Union. Perhaps that has something to do with the fact that the women still outnumbered the men in membership. In 1915 revenues were from "pew taxes, offerings, church collections, donations, calendars, sale of papers and old iron, the Ladies' Parish Society, the Social Circle, and the Catch and Give Society." Contributions were made to "the Girl Scouts, the Reed Fund, the B. B. Dixie Fund, the Lecraw Fund, and the J. J. H. Gregory fund."

The church was redecorated in 1914, new carpets being purchased from C. C. Bailey of Boston for $400, cushions from H. Coffin of Salem for $600, and a semi-indirect system of electric lighting for $450. Some people wanted to bring the old pulpit down from the attic, but the cost was deemed too expensive at $275 to $300. During the renovations the church was invited to use the facilities of the Unitarian church, a gesture which says much about the pleasant relations between the denominations in town. The Federal Council of Churches, created by 12 million Protestants in 1908 "to relate religion to society's problems," had helped to encourage this spirit of sharing.

And so we come to the year 1915. Let us look down again at this town and this church. In Marblehead, telephones ring, and where once the ear was lulled by the clop of horses' hooves on dirt, it is now startled by the roar of automobile engines and horns. Many houses burn brightly with electric light. The young people are going to the movies now. In fact, this new craze has become so popular that in 1915 the church sends a letter protesting the proposed showing of moving pictures on Sunday, saying that "we hold that the commercializing of the Christian Sabbath by such performance is against the public interest and would be detrimental to the moral and religious life of the community." The world has moved on, and there are as many decrying that fact as are embracing it.

Marblehead has managed to provide a common ground for the rich and the poor as well as those between. The First Church, now generally known as Old North, has grown from a membership of 220 members in 1910 to 232 in 1915. Now the daily newspapers report the terrifying rumbles of war which roll and reverberate across the sea until the ominous tide reaches our own peaceful, sail-dotted harbor.

Perhaps with war clouding the horizon and the recent prosperous times under threat, the church will remember the words of Pastor Nicholas Van der Pyl, who in his 1903 statement of belief expressed a desire "to make practical application of the spirit of God to the needs, sufferings and distressing problems of our human existence."

It is also to be hoped that, with the real threat from foreign enemies, Marblehead parishioners will somehow find the moral courage to resist prejudice and to retain their belief in the brotherhood of man, recognizing the truth that Nicholas Van der Pyl will state twenty years later, in 1935, that "Human nature is very much the same in any age."

9

The Best
and Worst of Times

NOVEMBER 7, 1918, was a day of rejoicing. False information about the armistice had turned the tensions of war into a day of revelry, and a parade was scheduled for that evening. A little girl happily hopped along with hand held tight and secure in her father's big warm one. The streets were filled with people looking forward to the parade.

At this very moment the little girl's secure world was shattered as smoke barreled skyward over the houses. Her father left like a runaway horse and ran toward the Burgess plant at Little Harbor. She stood confused and alone. It seemed as though fate had signaled the end of the war. For those dedicated workmen who had been frantically pushing out planes for the war effort, it was the end of high pay and steady employment. The fire destroyed the plant, and the airplane industry was gone from Marblehead. For the little girl it was to mean no more piano lessons or other goodies, for her father's big paycheck as foreman at the Burgess plant was exchanged for a low-paying job in Peach's laundry on State Street. He was more fortunate than the many who could find no work.

At war's end we had come to a new era in our outlook toward the future. We had won "the war to end all wars." New technologies developed during the war were producing longer and better automobiles; automatic heating was weaning us away from the coal shovel; and we were on the verge of dispensing with the iceman in favor of mechanical refrigeration for the home. The dots and dashes of Morse and navy codes were replaced

View from Abbot Hall circa 1915.

by voice communication over the airways. A spirit of optimism prevailed.

The veterans were gradually finding employment. Many harbored a resentment about Prohibition because they felt that while they were fighting for democracy the folks back home had taken away their freedom of choice regarding the use of alcoholic beverages. This, combined with the realization that those who had stayed behind were in much better shape financially, caused many to seek to catch up or their fortunes by rum-running. Marblehead, with its many islands and coves, had been a smuggler's paradise since the early days of the Stamp Act. This era was no exception.

It was under these condition that the Reverend Leslie Campbell Greeley shepherded his flock. Many present parishioners were tots in the Sunday school. A few present stalwart members of Old North were active church-goers and remember well the Burgess plant that, as the *Hannah* gave Marblehead the distinction of being the birthplace of the navy, so too did the Burgess plant pioneer the aircraft that contributed greatly to our newest branch of armed services, the U.S. Army Air Corps.

All in all, it was a time of challenge, a period of hope for better things to come. With this newfound optimism came an influx of engineers, scientists, merchandisers, and other middle-income people. They built homes throughout the farming area of Clifton. Many joined Old North and contributed to the growth and activity of the church.

In a victory sermon Rev. Leslie Greeley gave justification and consolation to those who so bravely fought the war to save democracy. He expressed justification to the participants and consolation to the heartbroken families whose sons made the supreme sacrifice that all wars demand. He quoted generously from St. Paul: "Thanks be to God which giveth us the victory through our Lord Jesus Christ."

Parts of his speech are worthy of thought to match the problems confronting us in today's world.

If a highwayman attacks us it is our duty to the highwayman, to ourselves and to society to defend ourselves up to the highest limit of our powers. Only so would a settled community be possible. But to suppose for a moment that conquering a highwayman by brute force is a real victory, is to give brute force a higher consideration than it deserves.

We need to keep these distinctions straight in war times. An era of brute force, under modern conditions, requires great cleverness in the construction of engines of destruction. We use these tools of destruction not because we like them, but because our enemies understand nothing else. . . . If a mad dog attacks we do not use the Ten Commandments or the Beatitudes upon him, but a pistol.

. . . It is not the highest kind of victory to drive a burglar out of the house. It is simply something which has to be done. But if in these days or in days to come we should fall into the error of glorifying war we should have surrendered to the very savage forces against which we are contending.

After the war, except in the case of many widows and fatherless children, life took on new enthusiasms. Church membership crawled to a modest gain each year.

The 1920s brought tremendous growth and change in harbor activities and yachting. Along with the passion for boating came a boom in building mansions on the Neck as well as housing developments in the Clifton area.

As the town grew, subtle changes took place in the church, partly from population growth and partly from the controversial issues of the times. These included the Volstead Act; woman suffrage; the new movie house; daring dress fashions; the increase in mechanical things such as washing machines, vacuum cleaners, electric refrigerators, and oil burners; and the increasing number of people who could afford automobiles.

The loss of industry was replaced by an influx of summer people. Attitudes changed along with new modes of living and employment and pro-

Typical lobster shanty on lower Front Street.

vided an abundance of sermon material for our ministers, who spoke about the abuses of our newfound freedoms.

One incident reflects the times as evidenced by the election of officers to the standing committee of the Society. Heretofore the records do not show women on this committee, but after the advent of woman suffrage in 1920 Mrs. Mary H. Ingalls became a member at the 1921 election of officers. It is interesting to note that during the period from 1918 to 1932 the same men were voted to serve on the standing committee of the church Society. There were additions, but only death deleted the original group. Again we see the significance of woman suffrage when, in 1920, the town's first public building to be named for a woman was the Mary A. Alley Hospital.

A letter dated May 16, 1922, was addressed to Mrs. Mary L. Goldthwait:

> Dear Madam: . . . your generous offer to present and install a new organ for the church was accepted unanimously. . . . Both the parish and the church are deeply gratified to you for your splendid gift, and it becomes my pleasant duty on behalf of each organization to officially thank you for the same.

A letter of thanks and acknowledgment of the organ recently installed was sent to Mrs. Goldthwait on January 16, 1923.

Apparently the effects of the new prosperity were being felt as the standing committee at a July 1923 meeting sanctioned the purchase of the baby grand piano from the Gregory estate for $375.

On a motion of Deacon Broughton made on June 10, 1923, it was voted that we adopt as a statement of our Christian faith the confession of faith which was adopted by the National Council of Congregational Churches covened at Kansas City in 1913.

On August 17, 1924, after fourteen years of service to our church, Rev. Leslie C. Greeley tendered his resignation.

My heart goes out to the people of Marblehead in affection and appreciation. The town with its noble history and great traditions has meant much to me. Our Christian labor together as pastor and people has been full of delight and has again and again been attended by results which have made our hearts glad. My prayer is that God may send his continued blessing upon you all. Cordially yours.

Dr. Harris G. Hale accepted the call to be our pastor on February 4, 1925, and eleven days later preached his first sermon for Old North. He wasted no time in familiarizing himself with the traditions and needs of the parish. From all comments by present parishioners who were old enough to remember, he was very well liked. Six months after his arrival he had organized an elaborate 100th anniversary service of rededication of the "Stone Church in Marblehead."

One of the controversies of the 1920s centered around the Scopes trial, a battle of lawyers attempting to resolve the differences between Darwinism and Fundamentalism. People everywhere were questioning whether a document created 2,000 and more years ago had validity in light of all the scientific discoveries in recent decades. Harry Emerson Fosdick, an outstanding theologian, wrote in 1925:

The old Book has moved into a new world. There are sharp contrasts between some ways of thinking in the Bible and our own. There is no use obscuring the fact. We would better set it out in the clear light and deal with it. For if we who are the disciples of the Lord do not do it in the interests of his people and his cause, it will be ruinously done for us by those who are his enemies.

On the recommendation of the music committee and approved by the standing committee during November 1925, the organ console was moved to the floor of the church.

The community life buzzed on, with more building, more yachts in the harbor, and the Rockmere Hotel making changes to meet the pressures of the times. Before the war summer resort hotels flourished throughout the ocean and mountain areas of New England. Vacationers would pack their trunks for stays varying from two weeks to the entire summer. Bag and baggage by train was the only way to travel, except that the more affluent were apt to arrive by carriage drawn by from two to four horses. As automobiles became more popular and more roads were paved to accommodate them, people moved around more freely and spent less time at any one place. This changed the hotel business considerably. Those that survived added ballrooms and big-name orchestras to attract dinner guests and transients to offset the loss of the all-summer patrons. Rockmere was no exception; all during the 1920s their "Fo'casle" with its gourmet dining and music was a popular place for the young and young at heart.

The church received a letter during August 1925 from the Christian Science Society requesting the use of our church facilities. The reply as written by Dr. Hale for the standing committee is testimony, not only of church policy at the time, but also to his tact in handling a refusal.

Although the Old North Church is Congregational in name, organization and affiliation, it is in fact unsectarian. Its teachings are undenominational. Therefore it is voted: That it would be unwise and inconsistent to allow its buildings to be used by individuals or organizations outside its own membership for lectures or other public meetings which have a distinct sectarian or denominational name or purpose and it was voted that a letter be sent to the Christian Science Society, declaring our position.

At a special meeting of the First Congregational Society held on February 7, 1927,

after some study and discussion of the financial condition of the Society and a tentative budget, showing the capacity of the Society's financial standing to absorb a proposed increase in salary without undue burden, it was voted: That the pastor's salary be increased to $2400. per year.

The vote was unanimous. In January 1929 the standing committee further increased the pastor's income by assuming $300 of the coal bill for the parsonage.

During the summer of 1929 the town held a three-month-long celebration to honor the 300 years since its founding in 1629. Each week had its special event, starting with opening exercises at Abbot Hall, followed by band concerts, historical exercises on Old Burial Hill, opening of old homes, a young peoples' parade, a harbor parade, harbor illumination, and fireworks. Other activities included a sports day, Sunday exercises, parade of floats with marching bands and military units, a portrayal in costume of Lafayette's visit to Marblehead, Saturday night dances, and a fireman's muster. These events brought tourists from far and near. It was one rousing, cheering event after another, not only celebrating the 300th anniversary of the town, but exemplifying the optimism of the times as well.

During the 1920s each year showed gains in the wealth of individuals, growth in the number of houses, and a population increase of 18 percent.

Optimism knew no bounds. Investors played the stock market with blind confidence that their fortunes would catapult to the millions. The less affluent and less knowledgeable for the most part banked their meagre savings. All the wild dreams of the Roaring Twenties came to a horrendous halt with the crash of the stock market in October 1929.

Marblehead proved a more stable community than most. Although there was hardship, the Marbleheaders helped each other. Many stories could be told of survival. Perhaps the executive with a Ph.D. who put pride aside and started a butter-and-egg route best describes the determination to "make it" without becoming another's burden. As business started its recovery there were many qualified applicants for each job offering. This writer recalls how a group of neighbors outfitted our butter-and-egg man when a job opportunity surfaced to match his skills. One man donated a business suit that was almost new. As it was too large, another friend tailored it to fit. Other neighbors supplied the money to finance the interview trip to New York City. Marbleheaders helping each other was a tradition. Interestingly enough, all the people involved were churchgoers but of different faiths. Old North was well represented. All through the following years of the depression such acts of Christian brotherhood brought out the best in people. It is unfortunate that the greatest acts of Christian charity, fellowship, and love go unrecorded.

Dr. Hale tendered his resignation on May 17, 1930. At a special meeting it was voted that he be given two months' additional salary beginning at the close of his pastoral duties. A letter addressed to "our dear minister" reads as follows:

It is with feeling of regret that we of the Parish of the Old North Church have accepted your resignation. The five years of your pastorate have been of the greatest help to us.

Old North interior in the late 1920s.

Through your suggestion the church is out of debt and you are leaving it stronger in membership than for years, especially in the number of young people who will carry on the work when we who are older have passed on.

We wish you and Mrs. Hale many years of health and happiness in your new home and are thankful that you both will remain Marbleheaders.

On Thursday, October 30, a year after the stock market crash, an ecclesiastical council met and proceeded to fulfill the requirements for the installation of the Reverend Dwight L. Cart as pastor.

From the start of his ministry at Old North Reverend Dwight Cart, like all preachers of the depression years, was confronted with the problems of unemployment, hunger, and privation among members of his parish. How to cure a sick business condition was uppermost in the minds of leaders from all walks of life. For the clergy it was the question of competence on the part of the spiritual order to help solve some of the suffering born of a bankrupt economy. From all accounts, the Reverend Mr. Cart met the challenge. He was an outstanding preacher and served the people of the parish well through the worst of times this country had experienced since the Civil War.

10

A Recovery of Vision

THE PERIOD from the mid-1930s through the mid-1950s saw many changes in the church, the town, and the nation. In the mid-1930s the Great Depression was in full swing; in the early 1940s the nation was involved in the bloodiest of wars; in the late 1940s recovery was under way; and by the 1950s economic and population booms were sweeping the country.

No community was immune to the effects of the depression, and Marblehead experienced considerable suffering, although not to the same extent as more industrial areas. In 1935 the ERA (Emergency Relief Administration) was providing temporary work for 110 men on drain projects and for 42 women on sewing projects, and in early 1936 over 200 men labored on WPA (Work Progress Administration) projects while 25 were employed by the PWA (Public Works Administration) in the construction of the first addition to the high school. At the same time, nearly 1,000 people were on welfare rolls.

These were the days when one considered himself fortunate if he had a regular job even though the hours worked may have been reduced below normal with corresponding reductions in pay. Wages were below starvation level by today's standards, with $30 to $35 per week considered good, but the cost of living was also low. An F. N. Osborne ad in September 1935 listed lettuce at 5 cents a head, butter at 25 cents a pound, two pounds of filled cookies for 25 cents, smoked shoulders at 21 cents a pound, and lamb chops at 29 cents a pound. Transportation also was a far cry from that of today: there were twenty-six trains a day between Marblehead and

Four former ministers of Old North and the incumbent at the 300th anniversary celebration on Old Burial Hill in 1935. From left: the Reverends Leslie Campbell Greeley, Dr. John Barrett, Dr. Nicholas Van der Pyl, Dr. Harris G. Hale, and Dwight L. Cart.

Boston with a fare of 64 cents for a round trip, or a commuter could purchase a monthly ticket for $12.14. A new Plymouth two-door sedan cost $550 delivered, and gasoline cost $1.00 for eight gallons. Streetcar service was available to Salem and to Lynn on a fifteen-minute schedule. Housing costs also were low. There were numerous ads for apartments in town from $15.00 to $25.00 per month; and, as an example of real estate values, the Tucker house (including a street-floor store) on Washington Street facing Darling Street sold for $3,500. It was in this bleak and uncertain atmosphere that Old North found itself in the mid-1930s. But it had survived and continued its ministries to the town through other trying times, and it had no intention of sitting down now; instead, it was determined to push ahead to even greater heights of service. As a rallying point the 300th anniversary of the gathering of the church was coming up in 1935, and a committee consisting of Rev. Dwight L. Cart, the senior deacon, and the chairman of the standing committee was elected in 1932 to plan appropriate observance of the occasion. There was also another significant event deserving of recognition — the 250th anniversary of the organization of the church as a Congregational church. Consequently, at its annual meeting on January 11, 1934, with 153 members answering the roll call, it was recommended by the 300th anniversary committee, and voted by the church, that the 250th anniversary of the organization of the church be suitably observed on August 12-13, 1934, and "that a committee consisting of the church committee and such members of the standing committee of the society who are not deacons . . . be the general committee to carry out the 250th anniversary plans."

The many subcommittees necessary to handle the several facets of the celebration and the scores of members whose help was required enthusiastically gave of their time and talents to create an appropriate observance of this significant event in the life of the church and the town.

On Sunday, August 12, at 10:30 A.M., morning worship with communion was led by Rev. Dwight L. Cart assisted by former ministers Dr. John W. Barnett, Dr. Nicholas Van der Pyl, and Rev. Leslie C. Greeley. This service was in observance of the 250th anniversary of the first service as a Congregational church held on August 13, 1684.

At 4:00 P.M. a service patterned after the form used in 1684 was held at Old Burial Hill with former ministers Dr. Harris G. Hale and Dr. Van der Pyl officiating.

On Monday, following a buffet supper in the parish house, a service was held in the sanctuary. Anniversary chairman Deacon Richard Tutt's introductory remarks were followed with a prayer by Dr. Barnett and greetings by William H. Wormstead, Dr. Joseph B. Lindsey, Dr. Joel E. Goldthwait, Hon. Malcolm L. Bell (chairman of the board of selectmen and son of former minister Rev. S. Linton Bell), and Rev. Roy M. Grindy (rector of St. Andrew's Church and president of the Marblehead Ministerial Association). The historical address was delivered by Rev. Leslie C. Greeley.

A historical paper, written by the Misses Ada R. Conway and Hannah Tutt, was read by Mr. Cart and was illustrated by the following tableaux:

"The Calling of Pastor Avery"
"Parson Walton Preaching to the Fisherman"
"Ordination of Parson Cheever"
"The Psalm" — Liner-out and Congregation repeating
"Blessing the Soldiers" — Parson Whitwell
"The Tithing Man"
"Founding the Sunday School" — Parson Dana
"Portrait of Parson Lawrence"
"Portrait of Parson Allen"

"Mrs. Williams and the Ladies' Aid"
"Portrait of Rev. S. Linton Bell and Bi-Centennial Hymn"
"The Church of the Future"
The reading and tableaux (in which over 100 characters were represented) were followed by the congregation singing "Marblehead Forever," which was written by Rev. Marcia M. Selman, a Universalist minister and member of Old North, who died in 1932. Benediction was pronounced by Mr. Cart. The outstanding event of the observation of the 300th anniversary of the gathering of the church was the restoration of the old pulpit and erection of the reredos behind it. In 1824, when the present church building was constructed, the beautiful mahogany pulpit which presently enhances the sanctuary was installed, as were the colonial-type box pews. However, when extensive repairs and renovations were performed in 1886, the box pews were replaced by the present ones, the pulpit was removed to the attic of the church, and an ornate reading desk and three large chairs were substituted. Fortunately, the original pulpit was not destroyed but was removed from the attic and carefully restored and dedicated to the memory of Rev. John Barnard.

From its organization as a Congregational church in 1684, Old North, as was traditional with Congregational churches, had been governed by two groups: The Church and The Society. In some areas the groups operated independently, and in others joint operation was required.

The Church, with the minister as moderator, and the deacons and deaconesses as a church committee, all under the direction of the church members, supervised programs and activities of the spiritual sector of the present-day church. On the other hand there was The Society, composed of pew owners who, nevertheless, were required to pay pew rental fees. Pew owners were not necessarily members of the church and were often not members of The Society. The Society, acting through its standing committee, was responsible for the maintenance of the physical property; the raising and expenditure of funds; and, in conjunction with the church, the selection and salary of ministers.

Under this form of government deacons, deaconesses, and members of the standing committee generally held positions for life, since there were no limitations on reelection. The negative effect of such a form of government became more and more apparent to those who sought greater participation and younger blood in the life of the church, and at the annual meeting of the church on January 15, 1942 (at which the charge for the dinner was 35 cents), a time between the pastorates of Rev. Oliver F. Wiese and Rev. Thomas A. Goodwin, the church voted "that the chair appoint

Marblehead Harbor by J.O.J. Frost, Marblehead resident and primitive painter of the 1930s.

a committee of three to act with a like committee from the society, to look into the matter of church incorporation and report at a later date." Appointed were Clinton A. Ferguson, Chester C. Parker, and George E. Nichols.

On February 2, 1942, it was unanimously voted to extend a call to Rev. Thomas A. Goodwin. The conditions offered and accepted were a salary of $2,700 per year, four weeks' vacation, and the use of the parsonage.

A meeting of the church, held on October 7, 1942, to hear the joint report of the committee on incorporation, voted "that this meeting, sitting as a committee of the whole, recommend that the church be incorporated and that these proposed by-laws be used as a basis for incorporation." On October 26, 1942, the proposed by-laws were discussed, amended, and approved, and it was voted that the church be incorporated under the laws of the Commonwealth of Massachusetts. On February 2, 1943, the church was incorporated, and the present form of government was adopted.

The rapid growth of the town, which commenced in the mid-1930s and continued into the 1970s, was felt by Old North with 277 new members added in the years 1936 to 1945, and 483 added during the years 1946 to 1955. This increase in membership also brought about an increase in church

Old North on a cold winter's night in the late 1950s or early 1960s.

school population resulting in severe overcrowding in the parish house. The overcrowding was so severe that it became necessary to have two sessions of school: one at nine thirty for older children, and the other during the church service for younger children so that parents could bring the children to school and also attend church.

Although it was recognized that no facilities could be constructed until after the end of the war, nevertheless the church wanted to be prepared when labor and materials would again be available. At the first meeting of the Church Council held under the new by-laws on March 5, 1943, one month after incorporation, it was voted "that a committee consisting of the pastor, moderator, and the senior deaconess take up the subject of remodelling the parish house and that they report on the nomination of two committees — one to look into the matter of plans, and one on the matter of financing." A month later the members of the two committees were nominated and elected.

The plans committee went to work immediately, but because of the small amount of land available the amount of ledge on it, and the committee's inability to acquire abutting land, progress was slow. Nevertheless, the architect did develop plans which met with the approval of the entire building committee and which were recommended to the church. These plans would have provided over three times the space of the then existing parish house. The brochure prepared for the church meeting stated, in part:

> The parish house shown here in plan and picture will truly be a home where all members of the community can find an opportunity to do the things they like to do whether it be sewing, dramatics, directing pageants, Scouting, square dancing, enjoying round table discussions on timely subjects, partaking of the sociability of a cup of tea or a real church supper or going to the chapel for quiet meditation.

A church meeting was held on December 3, 1945, to act on the recommendations of the building committee. After considerable discussion it was voted to refer the matter back to the building committee for further study and recommendations. The objection to the plans was that, because of the contours of the lot with its considerable ledge, it was necessary to have the auditorium on the second floor, making access difficult for the elderly.

A third architect was selected, and after the building committee again failed in its attempt to acquire more land, the plans for the parish house as it is today were developed. These general plans were approved at the annual meeting of the church on January 12, 1949, at which time it was also voted to proceed with a financial drive. A motion to obtain working drawings was laid on the table but finally approved on March 13, 1949.

In November 1949 Mr. Goodwin tendered his resignation to become executive secretary of the Minnesota Congregational-Christian Conference. A pulpit supply committee was formed, and on February 23, 1950, Rev. Robert S. Balfe was called. He took up the reins on March 16, 1950, and the church again turned its attention to a new parish house.

In July plans and working drawings were approved, and on September 27 it was voted "that the building committee be authorized to proceed with alterations and additions to the parish house, and that $86,000 be appropriated for said purpose."

Work began promptly and proceeded smoothly. Ledge was blasted from beneath the rear of the old parish house so that the auditorium floor could be dropped about five feet to its present level; the section containing the kitchen, central entrance, toilets, and parlor was constructed and tied through an existing window into the church; footing drains to direct water runoff from High Street were installed; a second floor was designed containing a chapel, classrooms, and office; and the section presently used by the younger pupils was erected out over the ledge. The job was completed by that fall, and on Sunday, November 4, 1951, it was duly dedicated.

The church has always endeavored to be a good neighbor extending a helping hand to those in need in Marblehead, in neighboring communities, in the United States, or anywhere in the world. Whether it was a conflagration in Boston in the 1700s, a devastating fire in Lynn in the 1980s, the destruction of the Maple Street Congregational Church in Danvers, or other catastrophes, the people of Old North rushed aid to help the victims. As an ongoing contribution to young people it sponsored Boy Scouts, Girl Scouts, Cubs, and Brownies. In 1951 Mr. William Hillman, a student at Andover-Newton Theological Seminary, was hired part time to oversee the church school and to work with youth groups, thus beginning an era of increased concern and attention to the youth of the church and the community.

Also in the 1950s, the church was supporting work at Bricks Rural Life School in North Carolina; the missionary efforts of Mr. and Mrs. John Scott in Talas, Turkey; and in 1953 it voted to give $1,000 a year for four years to the Congregational-Christian Church Building Loan Fund.

The rapid growth of the town in the late 1940s and 1950s was caused to no small extent by the many Jewish families moving into the Clifton area. There were no synagogues in town, nor, for that matter, any for the Reform followers in the immediate area. So when in 1954 the nucleus of Temple Emanu-El was formed in town it was invited to make use of the facilities of the new parish house. The offer was happily accepted, and the members of Temple Emanu-El Reform met at Old North until their synagogue was completed in 1959. The feelings of friendship and gratitude established during that period led to an invitation to the moderator of the church to participate in the ground-breaking ceremonies for the temple and to the dedication of one of its rooms to Old North. It was at this time that the joint Thanksgiving eve services, which are still being held, were inaugurated, and shortly after that an annual exchange of pulpits was commenced.

And so it was in this period that the church went through one of its greatest periods of growth, not so much in physical plant as in numbers of young, dedicated people who joined in the support of the church. Long-term objectives outlined by the church committee were to:

1. Work with prospective and new members, the sick, absent, and parish members in general to strengthen their spiritual life.

2. Integrate, or reintegrate, the various groups within the parish.

3. Make this church a living force for good within the community.

How well these objectives were achieved is reflected in the balance of this history as Old North faced a host of problems during the next two decades.

II

Unprecedented Growth

THE HISTORY OF the Old North Church and the affairs of Marblehead are so closely interwoven that one cannot look at the Old North of the 1960s without studying the community of Marblehead carefully. The problems of Marblehead in the 1960s were so demanding and complex that it found itself working at a distance from the nation as a whole, which was torn by civil strife and radical political activities.

Political analysts recording this national period refer to the 1960s in terms of the Chicago Seven, the Birmingham boycotts, the campus riots, the assassinations, the cries of forgotten people, and the ugliness of a war fought in living rooms through the miracle of television.

While Marbleheaders read and agonized, studied and lamented the nation's problems, the immediate concerns of expansion and population growth took precedence locally. It was in this decade of continued expansion that the ethnic and social composition of the town was to finalize radical change.

The 1950s saw an addition of 5,000 new citizens to Marblehead; the 1960s would record an additional 3,000 on population rolls. The 1950s had been a time for local building and planning: the schools, library, hospital, new police and fire stations stood ready to serve; the town had seen to these needs. Now these institutions were to be taxed beyond measure along with the recreational and religious organizations of a town suffering a population explosion. In 1969 the population reached 21,000.

What had caused this boom? Four factors:

1. Marblehead's geographical proximity to Boston and the rapidly expanding technological industries along Route 128 made the town a convenient bedroom community.

2. Marblehead provided a cosmetic attractiveness with narrow streets and historical charm, scenic vistas, and a beautiful harbor. (Who knew or cared about its northeast exposure to severe storms?) The promise of pleasant family recreation was implicit.

3. The families of the 1950s and 1960s were, in some cases, returned war veterans and, in other cases, young parents, college-educated in the 1950s. There was a "nesting instinct" as well as a belief that their economic fortunes were boundless. Believing that their good jobs would provide attractive homes and a comfortable lifestyle for their expanding families, they sought the strong schools, the parks, and the distance from urban dirt and noise.

4. The natives of Marblehead, suddenly aware of the town's desirability, became anxious to sell meadows here and back lots there. There was gold in every old pasture as local and out-of-town builders continued to fill the need for homes.

This was the community in which the Old North Church found itself. Although the growth spurt was common in many suburban communities across the United States, it is important to analyze local experiences in specific examples. The boom lasted twenty full years (longer than most, and it was to challenge a tightly organized community into shaping broader patterns of action).

Town reports and church reports provided the specific data of this chapter. The two sets complement one another and therefore should not be separated. However, for ease of reporting, this chapter will deal first with the total community, then with the Old North Church, which was straining to keep up with the demands for social changes caused by the arrival of so many "strangers" and their needs.

A graphic testament to the expansion fever is told by the number of articles for street layouts in the town warrants. Downtown there were Stoney Brook Road and Blueberry Road, and in midtown there were Girdler and Haley roads where cows had grazed. In the swamp on Atlantic Avenue across from Greystone came Greystone II with the names of presidents, and at Tent's Corner through to the West Shore Drive paraded new streets bearing college names. Mr. Sevinor, who had begun building in the 1930s in Clifton on the old Sirosis farm, continued with Thompson, Leo, and Sheldon roads, and off West Shore Drive on the Wyman land came Pinecrest Drive. There were additions to Beverly and Naugus avenues. One town employee recalls, "Hardly a day went by without requests for building permits. My God, I don't know how we kept up with it all."

To these houses came people with needs. The carefully planned schools of the 1950s were inadequate. The children of war veterans were growing, and youngsters moving into town needed education. School additions were approved year after year: two for the junior high school on Village Street, one at the high school and then the Bell School. Bond issues were a way of life. The school budget went from a scandalous $1 million plus to well over $2 million in the ten years.

Each town meeting contained requests for additional play space. Usher's Beach, between Devereux Beach and Goldthwaite Reservation, was purchased to make a "residents only" facility. The Homan land was purchased for a playground near the West Shore, and improvements were made at Gatchell's Pit. A football field was constructed behind the high school.

Each town meeting contained requests for additional policemen and fire fighters. There had to be new cruisers. Yearly the town meeting fought over the dump and over refuse collection. The incinerator, space for landfill, and the element of dump use brought crises.

With expansion came fear. There was the fear that the desire to turn dirt into gold had made the town less desirable. The town had acquired a large Jewish population. Between Marblehead and Swampscott there were four temples. With the synagogues which were built in town (Temple Emanu-El in 1959, Temple Sinai in 1962) came plans for a Jewish community center. Natives feared that the YMCA would be put out of business and that local religious observances would be curtailed.

This fear erupted in December 1969 into a series of community demonstrations to protest the school department's removal of religious symbols and religious music during the Christmas season. This decision was made because of a sensitivity toward the large number of Jewish children in the system. Feeling fear of different beliefs and a loss of tradition, numbers of citizens picketed the home of the superintendent of schools. The town received coverage in national news magazines. The nonsectarian celebration of the holiday remained, and Marblehead settled down, unsure just what the issue had been. Hanukkah celebrations became part of the school holiday festivities as well.

There was the fear that Marblehead would have too many apartments, and each town meeting brought renewed fights to protect the character of the community. The historic district, to protect the historical authenticity of Precinct 1, was accepted in the 1960s after a long, hard battle on the town meeting floor.

The most remarkable fight of the 1960s was the confrontation over the Rockmere property on Gregory Street, site of the once famed resort hotel. Countless months of study went into a proposal to turn the land at Skinner's Head into a town recreation facility. In the end, the town turned down the option, and Glover Landing, a condominium development, was built in 1965.

Marblehead, fearing that its open land would all disappear, set up a conservation commission in the 1960s, trying to buy up wetlands and to encourage tax deductible donations of land with unspoiled vegetation for relief from street after street of house lots.

Additions to the Mary A. Alley Hospital were defeated for financial reasons and because of the proximity of Salem Hospital, and Marblehead babies had to be born in Salem. The maternity space was converted to a floor for general medical and surgical treatment. Another fear became vocal: Would Marblehead lose its character and individuality completely? The last real Marbleheader had been born!

Social change always brings confusion, uncertainty, and fear. Real or imaginary, these fears were part of the climate surrounding Old North in the 1960s.

At the Old North Church the 1960s began on a low note. The church membership declined, showing a net loss of five members for the year 1960, and failed to meet its budget needs by $16,000. The Reverend Eric Rickard resigned, and the Reverend Franklin Cole, D.D., became interim pastor. Meanwhile, Mr. Stephen Bonta left as organist.

As the church awaited its next minister, one could feel a new era at hand. The church needed fresh ideas and rebirth, as Old North had some growing to do. Marblehead's population had expanded by 5,000 people in the past decade, and the challenge lay clear at Old North. The Reverend Kendall Link, assistant minister, wrote in his 1960 annual report that outreach was a need, and he urged that each member "become his own minister." He wanted more calling to begin through a lay ministry. Rev. Kendall Link was concerned with community needs, and his deep interest in the number of young adults in the community without a church home motivated the formation of the "W.P.'s" (Working People), designed to serve this specific age group. This group continued successfully even after the Reverend Link's resignation in 1961. As the 1960s progressed, serving the young adults became a matter of concern in all Marblehead churches,

The Social Circle prepares a chowder in the 1950s.

and a Young Adult Interchurch Fellowship was formed so that working and college-affiliated young adults from all denominations could meet for spiritual contact and recreation. This concern for the needs of young adults was the first of many interfaith activities in which Old North would acknowledge the changed complexion of Marblehead and would affirm a desire for cooperative effort to meet community needs. The group continued successfully for seven years.

The Reverend George M. Hooten, Jr., D.D., was called to Old North in 1961. Dr. Hooten and his wife, Evelyn, came to the church from a successful pastorate in Manchester, New Hampshire. Their grown daughter, Kathy, already independent, did not accompany them. Dr. Hooten preached eloquent and very dramatic sermons, and he brought with him a sense of the challenge ahead. His ministry would encompass the entire decade, bringing a stability of focus.

Several more programs developed from the need to reach out to newcomers of all faiths and to learn who were neighbors. The new people in Marblehead needed churches, and Dr. Hooten began his ministry by organizing a group called The Fishermen to become "fishers of men" in the biblical sense. Meeting new people, touching new families, and drawing these people to Old North was the goal. Each year of the 1960s brought a net gain in membership growth. The church moved from a membership of 1,046 to a recorded figure of 1,310 in the decade. Dr. Hooten added special classes for those joining the church to better explain our beliefs to those coming to us from a variety of denominations.

Dr. Hooten was anxious to reach as many families as possible and to accommodate as many lifestyles as the church could serve. During fall, winter, and spring months one Sunday each month was designated Family Sunday, and Sunday school children joined their parents in the sanctuary. The aim was to strengthen families through church participation.

Under the leadership of Virginia Webber the church offered a vacation Bible school program for a week or more each summer of the 1960s. The attendance grew each year.

Daily nursery schools, housed but not sponsored by churches, sprang up all over town, and Old North had its nursery school successfully directed by Mrs. Roger Fowler of Old North. These nursery schools showed church cooperation in serving needs of the young, affluent families who were enjoying Marblehead and its lifestyle. Again, "family" is the key word. Marblehead and Old North were hearing their needs.

Dr. Hooten brought attention to a need to acquire property. He knew that the "locked-in" facilities on Washington Street offered no room for

The sanctuary at Christmas in the 1950s.

expansion, and he saw the increasing population of Marblehead as a mandate for plant growth. So the trustees of Old North, with the approval of the church members, began land acquisition. In 1963 the church became the owner of property at 1 Pearl Street, 8 Stacey Street, and 49 Washington Street. Before the decade ended, the church acquired property at 8 Pickett Street as a bequest from Wilhemina Denning Jackson and then sold it. It also acquired additional property on Stacey Street and the Parson Barnard House on Franklin Street with sufficient land to assure parking for Old North's expanding needs. The property at 49 Washington Street and at 1 Pearl Street provided housing for Religious Education Director Virginia Webber, who served the entire decade, and for the Reverend Ralph Short, who served as assistant minister from 1962 until 1965. Rev. Ralph Short came from Andover-Newton Theological Seminary and was ordained in the sanctuary. During his time at Old North he met June Fagg, a parishioner, and they were subsequently married and lived at 49 Washington Street. Additional space for nursery classes and a youth room were provided at 1 Pearl Street.

It is ironic that the one piece of property which the church so anxiously desired remained elusively unattainable. This disappointment was recorded in the words of Donald Daley, chairman of the trustees, in 1968. The property in question was 43 Washington Street, and Mr. Daley concluded:

The land and building appeared to be very desirable as a present and/or future addition to our physical plant and the purchase was considered sound.... However, before a special church meeting to consider the purchase [required by the by-laws] could be convened, the property had been sold.

Needless to say, Mr. Daley suggested by-law changes! Thus, the real estate acquisitions may be seen as one answer to the growth problems.

Serving youth! This was a primary concern at Old North. The Sunday school enrollment kept constant almost through the decade at about 400 youngsters. Under the leadership of the Reverend Ralph Short, at one point there were 50 members in the youth group. The Rev. Mr. Short called extensively throughout the community attempting to reach teens who needed a viable church contact.

These booms in attendance lasted until almost the end of the decade when a decrease in Sunday school enrollment was noted (one year 4 percent, another 2 percent). This slight decline was of concern to Dr. Hooten, and in his annual report for 1969 he suggested that midweek church services with a church school session might become a way to better serve the congregational needs. The more affluent families were skiing in the winter, and church attendance was suffering. This idea was not successfully implemented.

It was difficult for a hardworking church to see attendance figures drop, and there were many causative factors. The "good life," so eagerly sought by new young families of the 1960s, had included church attendance, but the pressures of suburbia, jobs, and family living tensions were causing problems in many homes. Working mothers (inflation had begun) needed Sundays at home, and as the economy pressured, church attendance was dropping nationally. Many were sensitive to the climate of the 1960s with its unrest and national strife, and they felt that the churches were not responding to these problems with programs and action for the troubled times.

Since so many of the problems of the 1960s (and, indeed, through the 1980s) were domestic, the number of cases of counseling handled by the ministers grew with the problems of the decade. In 1969 Dr. Hooten recorded 123 counseling sessions, and Rev. Charles Francis Hood, associate minister since 1965, reported 27 cases with 61 sessions. Personal distress calls had become a way of life.

The Reverend Charles Francis Hood joined Old North in 1965, having previously served as minister of Immanuel Congregational Church in

Beverly. Because of commitment to a large and growing family, he and his new wife, Dolly, kept their Beverly home. A man for all seasons, he served the youth group, taught the pastor's class, and made extensive calls on the sick and infirm. He was, and is, chaplain to fire departments, a master chef; and, as a prestidigitator, has performed his magic tricks at many social occasions.

Interfaith youth work in Marblehead was followed by a Brotherhood Council which worked on plans affecting the entire spiritual community of Marblehead, such as the community brotherhood award and the Thanksgiving eve services which reaffirmed the friendship and shared beliefs with Temple Emanu-El, Jewish neighbors who had used the new parish house while their temple was being built.

The Rosenfield family visited the Sunday school on several occasions to explain Jewish customs, and the children were treated to a program by Dr. Murray Nichol, head of the Semitic Museum at Harvard. Interfaith awareness and respect was a goal.

Mr. Hood was active in a North Shore Ecumenical Council, and Virginia Webber, who was very positive in her desires for outreach to blacks, did volunteer tutoring with needy black children in Lynn and included them in the summer vacation Bible school programs in the late 1960s. Marblehead was trying to overcome its fears by celebrating common beliefs and interests, and the Old North Church provided personnel and leadership for many community and outreach ventures.

What else was Old North about in the decade? It was a busy, active church. Its music program grew and flourished. Its organist, Stephen Bonta, left to be replaced by David Fuller and then by Mrs. Evelyn Faucher. The church was saddened at the resignation of Marie Vaughan, who had served as soloist for so many years. In 1966 Mrs. Lois Genis was welcomed as organist and choir director, and in 1967 she led the choir in a superb rendition of Gabriel Fauré's Requiem. Plans were afoot for reconditioning or replacing the organ, and there were four professional soloists by 1969: Carl Bratt, Catherine Oram, Paul Simpson, and Elisabeth Tierney.

Church fairs were continually expanding in features offered and in the profit realized. Many women worked diligently on these fairs, and under the leadership of Mrs. Robert Baker over $3,000 was raised in 1968. Mrs. William Rodenbaugh continued the tradition in 1969.

It is not possible to name all dedicated laypersons for these years, but there is so much consistency of leadership by a few that some names have to be mentioned. Evelyn Ohm probably gave more hours than any other church member between her work in the choir and her service as church financial secretary. Arthur R. Magee served as church treasurer for most of the decade, and John H. Ferguson was moderator for the entire span. Mrs. Samuel Gray and Mrs. William Riley brought beauty to the sanctuary with ten years as flower chairmen, and Wilson H. Roads served as historian. The professional staff was remarkably stable: Dr. Hooten, Virginia Webber, and from 1965 the Reverend Charles Francis Hood, whose dedicated service has been era-spanning. The Reverends Mr. Link and Mr. Short had but a few years at Old North. Mrs. Charles H. Learoyd worked as a dedicated church secretary, often in a highly executive capacity.

No history of the Old North Church would be complete without referring to the theft of the beautiful and historical sacramental silver in 1969, an act that shocked the entire community. The church was gratified that so many people donated new pieces so generously. However, as the 1960s ended, Old North was still hoping for a break in the case. (For the complete account of this unfortunate affair, see "Our Heritage Communion Silver" which is included in the appendices.)

The church met a modest Christian Service budget each year, but 1969 showed a remarkable breakthrough with a special pledge of $18,000 for Mission Advance, this money being allocated for the troubled urban situations throughout the nation. The Old North supported the Reverend and Mrs. John Scott, teaching missionaries in Turkey, making it feel closer to the Congregational church in its worldwide mission.

A history of any organization is of "hails and farewells," and no farewell was more poignantly grateful than that to the Social Circle. For years these ladies were a strong force in the church, providing fellowship for their members and for the church as a whole. In 1964 the club of then senior citizens stopped meeting, having been together since girlhood. In 1961 the club recorded twenty-five meetings and they still had twenty-one members, but failing health made continuing an impossibility. One thinks with awe of the number of suppers, fair tables, and missionary projects these women provided.

Social and service groups otherwise remained strong: The World Friendship Guild, the Y-Con Club, the S.O.S. Club, and two couples' clubs.

As the 1960s ended, one saw a portrait of a church truly trying. There was confusion about the beginning of a decline in attendance and a drop in Sunday school enrollment. Old North had never really balanced a budget during this period; nevertheless, many important milestones mark the passage of these years: the ecumenicity and outreach challenges met by the church, the acquisition of properties which would prove themselves financial assets, and the expansion of services.

As the 1960s gave way to the 1970s, many questions remained about the effectiveness of the community mission. The same questions faced the town. How could Old North further facilitate cooperative living and effectively maintain dialogue and warm relations with so many new citizens? Marblehead's growing pains were really not over. The answers seemed slow in coming.

12

The 1970s

THE HISTORY of Old North Church during the first eight years of the 1970s is marked by striking contrasts and contradictions. On the one hand, the church experienced tremendous growth and change; on the other hand, the church experienced decline and frustration. Ironically, in some respects, the two apparently contradictory postures went hand in hand or, in some cases, were a product of one another.

The social and political forces which were shaping the country as a whole during the 1970s were not widely felt at Old North. The congregation was in no way nearly as divided or as scarred by the war in Vietnam as was much of the general population. Both protest and support were left primarily to the conscience of the individual. The Watergate scandal of the early 1970s found its way into sermons from the pulpit as the Reverend George Hooten likened the corruption of ancient Israel to the corruption we were viewing in Washington. But again, there was no ground swell of either protest or support from within the church. That, again, was left to the individual, and in some instances Old North became the recipient of members of other churches where these controversial issues had become divisive.

But, in other ways, social and political forces of the times had a profound influence on the church. Old North, more harshly than most of its individual congregants, felt the effects of runaway inflation in the mid-1970s. The disaffection and mistrust of social institutions and authority, wrought largely by Vietnam and Watergate, insinuated themselves into the workings of Old North as attendance and support declined (as they did in most churches nationwide during this period). Finally, the effects of what has been called the "Me" generation (infiltrated by many generations) changed attitudes about what was expected from ministry at Old North.

Two significant events introduced the 1970s, events arguably outside the person-to-person ministry of the church, yet events which might well have more long-range importance in the history of the church than the work of any individual in the church. The first of these events was the return of the church's heritage silver after protracted negotiations between Dr. Hooten and an intermediary and the payment of a sizable ransom, as detailed in the appendices.

The second event which introduced the 1970s is not nearly as intriguing as the silver heist but, on a week-to-week basis, probably has had more effect. That event was the refurbishing of the worship center of the church. Visitors seeing our sanctuary for the first time often comment on its "Federal" appearance. They admire its clean lines, its symmetry, its lack of ostentatious ornamentation. Members before 1970 and those who have seen photographs of the older sanctuary realize that this "Federal" appearance reached its present state little more than a decade ago. In 1958 the organ, which in the 1920s replaced a smaller organ located at the level of and to the right of the pulpit, was moved to a newly built organ chamber behind the wall of the church. The choir level was dropped to the level of the lower platform, and the console remained at floor level.

But time had taken its toll of this organ, and after considerable study the members of the church voted to purchase a new instrument and install it in the balcony. Space and weight requirements necessitated the rebuilding and strengthening of the balcony, and this led to the transformation of a small, three-stairway vestibule into a more spacious, well-lighted narthex in which parishioners could greet one another and the clergy before and after services. The tracker organ, one of the best of its kind in the Boston area, was built and installed by Aeolian Skinner at a cost of approximately $75,000. It was dedicated on October 17, 1971, and was paid for by special pledges and contributions from the congregation. The removal of the choir platform and the organ console from the front of the sanctuary achieved the present striking symmetry.

New carpeting was laid, and the four unattractive and inefficient hanging bowl lights were replaced by unobtrusive recessed lighting. Through the generous gift of Mrs. Malcolm L. Bell the graceful chandelier now seen hanging in the center of the room and the sconces on the rear wall were installed.

These changes present the worshiper with images of beauty, grace, and simplicity and offer generations of worshipers to come an aesthetic sanctuary as well as a spiritual one.

These one-time special events of the early 1970s take on an importance above and beyond the time in which they occurred because their effect is so long range and ongoing. But in their midst the day-to-day life of the church operated to provide a more temporal history.

The key element which influenced Old North Church in the early 1970s was the formation of a new ad hoc committee in the church — the Triple C Committee which for the first time brought together representatives of all the major committees of the church to meet regularly with the ministers of the church for the purpose of Communication between the various leaders within the church, Coordination of efforts in an attempt to reduce wasted energy and resources, and Change through the various offices open to the church.

Although the Triple C Committee was without an official role in the church, its clout shaped the early 1970s at Old North through two important facets of church life: youth ministry for the present and strategic planning for the future. While both of these contributions point to the strength of the church in the early 1970s, they were ironically to be in part related to some of the problems which were to develop later in the decade.

Youth ministry at Old North had long been a concern of the church. The church employed a full-time director of Christian education, but responsibilities for youth work usually fell to the associate minister who already had more than enough duties and responsibilities to keep him busy. Increasing numbers of teenagers in the church family, plus increasing awareness of the problems facing young people in the 1960s and 1970s, finally moved the church to action. Under the direction of the Triple C, funds were raised to hire a part-time minister to youth in the fall of 1971, Eugene Arnould, then a student at Harvard Divinity School (and a United Methodist). The following year, Virginia Webber tendered her resignation after many years of loyal service as director of Christian education, and Mr. Arnould was called to be Old North's first minister to youth and education.

The years that followed could well be called the "era of youth ministry" at Old North Church. The church provided space in its property at 1 Pearl Street for a youth room where Gene Arnould met regularly with senior high youth. Less regular sessions were held with junior high school youth. Dances for teenagers were held in the parish hall. Although Mr. Arnould continued to meet with young people on a weekly basis, he came to see

Old North from Washington Street.

his ministry calling him to greater activity with young adults and adults throughout the community.

A combined effort of both young and older members of the church family under Mr. Arnould's direction produced a worship series called New City in the spring and winter of 1972. New City was an experiment in contemporary worship (which were 1970 code words for folk or rock music, multimedia, and increased "relevance" in the worship experience). Participants met each Tuesday night to plan the following week's service scheduled for the eleven o'clock time slot after the formal hour of worship.

Mr. Arnould also organized a theater group in the church, the Golden Cod Players, which from 1972 to 1975 produced *J.B.*, *Inherit the Wind*, and *Sandburg* in the sanctuary. Actors for the productions came from throughout the community as well as from the church.

Just a few months before he left his position at Old North to pursue graduate studies in Indiana, the church celebrated with Mr. Arnould his ordination as a minister in the United Church of Christ.

Howard ("Skip") MacMullen replaced Mr. Arnould as minister to youth and education in 1975. Skip, a Yale Divinity School graduate, brought with him an emphasis on the church's spiritual dimensions as opposed to Mr. Arnould's more worldly concerns. Skip began his ministry at Old North by implementing an eight-year curriculum for the church school which he had designed and tested himself. He initiated opportunities for adult education within the church through several Bible study groups and through special Lenten programs which looked at the works of Christian writers and philosophers like C. S. Lewis and Morton Kelsey. His workshops with small groups of persons within the church helped individuals to develop deeper understandings of their faith and of their Christian potential. It was his initial introduction of Morton Kelsey's work which eventually led to the founding of the Companions of the Way group.

In his minstry to youth, Skip enlisted the services of Ray Hilwig, who took over primary responsibility for work with junior high youth.

Skip's wife, Flo, was an active participant with him in his work. Flo also was active with women in the church and, in 1976, was a founding member, along with Linda Marcy, of Amity Circle, a new group in the church designed to provide a place for younger women in the church to meet. Skip and Flo left Old North in 1978 to accept a position in Connecticut.

The other major contribution of the Triple C Committee was the implementation of strategic planning in 1971 under the direction of Richard C. Harrison III. The goal was to restate the goals and objectives of the Old North Church in contemporary terms, and to suggest by-law changes and organization changes if necessary. Perhaps the most significant contribution of the planning process (like the Triple C Committee itself) was the relatively massive infusion of lay participation in the formulation of church policy and direction, a task heretofore left largely to the clergy, even in the Congregational tradition.

The church newsletter, *Inspiration*, was born during this period under the editorship of Harold and Julia Bantly and Richard and Betty Perelli. This was also the era of the church fair at Old North. A holiday fair had long been a tradition at the church; however, fair chairmen broke all records in the early 1970s in terms of both the social as well as the financial success of the events.

The year 1974 saw Old North Church history made as women began to serve communion to parishioners for the first time. Prior to this women's role in terms of communion was relegated to preparation and cleanup. A few objected to the practice, but the change was overwhelmingly embraced by women and men alike who felt generally, "Why not before?"

Unfortunately, during this period Old North also saw the demise of several adult fellowship groups which had been a part of the church for many years (e.g., the Co-weds club and the Men's Club), and the Sunday morning worship schedule dropped from two formal services to one.

Two other significant events outside the control of the church were to greatly affect it during the latter part of this period: the first was the death of Mrs. Hooten in 1974; the second was the Arab oil embargo and its subsequent effect on the economy of this country.

Mrs. Evelyn Hooten, a woman of tremendous southern charm and wit, had suffered for years with an aggravated deterioration of bones in her neck. In her last years all efforts to relieve her pain were fruitless, and she spent most of her time confined to bed. After her death in July 1974 the church suffered with Dr. Hooten the loss of his wife.

The other event affecting Old North during this time was the incredible inflation which hit the American economy after the Arab oil embargo in the early 1970s. Always on a no-fat budget, prices for church "goods" (supplies, heat, repairs) skyrocketed as church giving leveled off. Attempts at saving money by moving church offices to 10 Stacey Street helped to some extent, but in 1975 the church budget was still underfunded by pledges. Capital reserves began to be used, and some of the investment property accumulated through the late 1960s was sold to aid cash flow.

Thus, two events kicked off by the Triple C Committee in a time of growth and enthusiastic change came to head in the mid to late 1970s to form crises. First, given unforeseen economic troubles, the salary for a third full-time minister was a luxury the church could not afford, regardless of how much it was wanted. When Skip MacMullen resigned in 1978, it was decided that the position should not be refilled.

Second, the increasing participation of the laity in the church and its policymaking gave church leaders a greater sense of their own power. This sense of lay responsibility, fostered and nurtured by the ministerial staff on the one hand, finally came into conflict with the authority of the minister on the other hand.

After a seventeen-year ministry at Old North Church, George Hooten retired in the fall of 1978. His ministry had seen the church grow and prosper as it never had before. Property was developed for generations to come.

Yet his ministry also saw social events take their toll on this congregation. George Hooten left a legacy of intellectually sound and stimulating preaching and a theological perspective which made our church ecumenically, racially, and politically open. The church had been challenged to understand that protest against whatever claims ultimate authority for itself is at the root of our liberal Protestant tradition.

As Old North moved into a new era and looked forward to the coming of a new minister, one final challenge remained from Dr. Hooten's final annual report to the church (1977) which church members of any era would do well to heed: "I'm sure Old North Church will continue to exist. It has shown remarkable staying power through the years and through adversity. But the question is not existence. It is quality of ministry by the whole church."

13

A View of the Present

T HE OCTOBER EVENING was clear and crisp. It felt good to gather around the warmth of pot-luck and conversation. After supper the eleven members of Old North's appraisal and search committee and the ministerial candidate who had come for the interview sat around Peg Munro's big dining room table. The committee had met many times since its formation the previous January at the church's 1978 annual meeting. Elected to represent various interests within the church, they had directed an intense process of self-study by the congregation as a whole. Responding to what was felt to be a "critical financial situation and our diminishing congregation," the appraisal process resulted in the identification of three goals for the near future: (1) balancing the budget; (2) more lay involvement in the entire spectrum of church life; and (3) fulfilling a commitment to the youth of the church through the organization of a variety of programs.

Bob Gotschall, chairman of the committee, addressed Ran Niehoff and proceeded to list the personal qualities the church was looking for in a new senior minister (the last one mentioned provides a key to understanding the latest period in the history of the First Church of Christ in Marblehead).

Well-educated yet still engaged in learning; neither strongly conservative nor strongly liberal in theological viewpoint; dynamic and effective preaching; energetically concerned for pastoral care; advocate of lay involvement; developer of Christian Education programs for all ages; mature, with a sense of humor, and

112

with an ability to live with diversity of opinion and work well with staff and lay leaders; able to walk on water in summer as well as in winter!

In the interim period between senior ministers a consensus had emerged that a congregation's health does not depend upon the gifts of a particular clergyman. There was a fresh awareness that the ministry of the church was free to draw on the insight and energies of the whole congregation. Although Mr. Gotschall's list turned out to be a fair description of Dr. Niehoff's personality, what is more important is the fact that it was also a fair description of the *personality of the church.* Throughout the following winter, stabilized by the teaching and pastoral calling of the Reverend C. Francis Hood ("Rev. Charlie"), and guided by the organizational skills and good humor of the Reverend Richard Borngen ("interim minister"), the church began to grow internally and externally. Upon Dr. Niehoff's arrival in April 1979, enthusiasm was the prevailing mood in the life and work of Old North Church.

Although life is inspired by faith before it is recorded by statistics, a quick look at numbers reveals that the three goals articulated in 1978 were realized: the church budget was balanced by 1980; average Sunday attendance grew from 161 in 1978 to 251 in 1983 (with more than 140 individuals holding positions of leadership in the congregation); and enrollment increased from 115 to 267 in Sunday school and from 26 to 50 in youth fellowships. When one reviews the life of a community, one sees that numbers may not be so important but that trends are. Viewed within the larger context of some of the indentifiable historical trends of the late 1970s and early 1980s, the growth in Old North provides an insightful perspective on the current personality of this grand old church:

. . .While the nation's economy agonized with the "dis-ease" of both inflation and recession by tightening budgets, the trustees and stewardship committee sought and received pledging from parishioners that outpaced the inflation rate, empowering the church's life with more "real" dollars each year.

. . .While the care givers in America pointed out more and more instances of a national "hardening of the heart" toward the disadvantaged, the Christian service committee administered a growing sum of money provided by church people as an expression of Christian caring (the proportion of pledges given for mission and outreach grew from 14 percent in 1978 to 21 percent in 1983).

. . .While the news media became more proficient at bringing home disturbing issues of the world with instantaneous urgency (specially con-

Colonial costumes at Marblehead's 350th anniversary celebration.

cerned to excite us with sensational depictions of tragedy), the church's mission projects became more effective because of patient research, strategic giving, and "hands-on" contact with human need (specially concerned to excite us with a sensational awareness of our power to help).

. . . While the private home became better equipped and its occupants more inclined to stay there for comfort and entertainment, Old North's lay leaders renewed their efforts to invite folks out to gather in groups of all sizes for fellowship and work.

. . . While Western technology forged ahead polishing elite tools and professional specialists for every task, the church in Marblehead returned whenever possible to the Old World/Early Frontier custom of asking the blue-collar and the white-collar worker, student and retiree, male and female to pitch in at work bees rather than "hire out" the job.

. . . While most casual conversations in suburbia included a kind of moaning about how busy everyone seemed to be, church business required and received more time from people of all ages.

. . . While public perceptions about the value of classical and sacred music grew fuzzier and popular music dominated the curricula of elementary and secondary music education, the music committee committed the congregation to the disciplined exposure of formal training in sacred music.

. . . While modern organizations relied more on mass communications techniques, the church relied more and more on the most respectful way to engender human response — person-to-person contact.

. . . While it was documented that on the whole only "conservative churches" were growing in the United States, this Yankee church maintained its historic resistance to allowing biblical faith to be boiled down into a set of man-made dogmatic propositions created by a cultural mood swing.

. . . While many religious groups bent on institutional survival caved in to the temptation to apply "crowd management" techniques practiced by manipulative secular managers, this assembly, steeped in town-meeting-style Congregational democracy, refused to try to persuade with either promise or threat.

. . . While organizations from the local club to one's alma mater found new sources of funding by appealing to the guilt of prospective supporters, the First Church in Marblehead tried to focus on how its work affected people and simply asked potential donors to join in the work, freely and cheerfully.

. . . While individuals in all segments of American society discovered the exhilaration of rallying which accompanied the growing phenomenon called "one-issue politics," the Marblehead congregation recognized the danger of self-righteousness on either extreme and wisely refrained from trying to force consensus, welcoming members from diverse backgrounds and encouraging divergent points of view.

. . . While the turbulent atmosphere of economic instability and the pace of social change precipitated the release of frustration, cultivating seeds of bigotry that had seemed to have been lying dormant (e.g., the rise of the Ku Klux Klan, neo-Nazi groups, anti-Semitic "jokes" and vandalism, racial tension), Old North joined with all the churches and temples in Marblehead to reaffirm the biblical covenant of "loving your neighbor as you love yourself" and the American constitutional guarantee of "freedom of worship and assembly."

. . . While most organizations established endowment funds primarily for purposes of self-preservation, Old North chose to invest the major portion of a new 350th Anniversary Endowment Fund into an expansion of its local service and an extension of its mission outreach.

. . . While Americans from every ethnic origin took up the fastest-

A summer Sunday service at Lighthouse Point in 1983.

growing hobby since Monday night football — genealogy — moved in part
by the sense of personal uniqueness aroused when one's roots are stroked,
the church has gone further than restoring and displaying its precious archives as an exercise in pride: it began its 345th year by leading a memorial
service at Old Burial Hill where, with the help of children representing
all the religious congregations in town, flowers were placed on the graves
of townspeople from Marblehead's first century; and the church plans to
celebrate its 350th year by involving the town in events which mark the
faith and tolerance nurtured here by the religious heritage of *all* the
congregations.

It is interesting to note that only with hindsight can one see the differences between societal trends and the church's countertrends over the
past five years. During that period not a word was spoken about *trying*
to buck trends, nor did anyone reveal a burning desire to achieve the appraisal's stated goals for his or her own sake. Such motives would have
been symptoms that the church had fallen prey to the worship of the "god-
dess 'success' " (which William James called "our national disease"). The
people of Old North Church achieved their goals, not because they were
trying to be successful, but because they were trying to be *faithful*.

In the New Testament the Greek word for "church" is *ekklesia* (which means "called out from"); the four functions for which a congregation is called out from the world to become a church is introduced by these four biblical terms:

1. *kerigma* — telling/teaching the story (*evangelion*) of God's saving actions in history, especially as revealed in the life of Jesus the Christ;

2. *diakonia* — serving/ministering to others, meeting needs and helping;

3. *koinonia* — sharing in fellowship, holding life in common as companions;

4. *latreuo* — working together to make life worth-full, doing worship.

Following are some of the special events that occurred in the life of a parish determined to be a church.

Kerigma

For the story of God's interaction with people to be told, for the Judeo-Christian ethic of love to be taught, there must be "two or three gathered together" — and that means there must be a place to meet and an agenda planned whereby people can take turns talking and listening. Lots of energy, physical and mental, has been invested in providing the places and sparking the conversations.

There is fresh paint everywhere, inside and out, from top to bottom. The elegant tower has been regilded in gold leaf, as has the codfish weather vane which has been in use since 1695. Volunteer crews have repainted the pews and great windows and shutters in the sanctuary and redecorated the parlor in "Federal" good taste. The parish hall classrooms sport bright colors to alert the senses. In the fall of 1982 Gordon Smith completed the whimsical, delightful mural in the nursery which depicts familiar biblical themes.

Determined to make incarnate the spirit of the theme "that all may enter," the congregation completed a series of projects during the early 1980s that resulted in the permanent, tasteful installation of access ramps and an electric lift plus a parking lot doubled in size. Plans are under way to utilize more fully the offices and rooms at 10 Stacey Street to make the old saltbox more accommodating for varied purposes from housing archives to overnight guests, counseling to classes, mailings to meetings — all in the tradition of hospitality for which the historic property has been known since the 1680s when it served as a tavern through the 1800s when it became a frequent hiding place of the Underground Railroad. Hospitality to worship even extends out-of-doors; a unique trait of the parish is a fondness for holding early services at the Marblehead lighthouse in the summer and on Old Burial Hill every Easter sunrise.

Once a group has gathered, the preaching/teaching can begin. Church groups gather in as many places as there are reference Bibles placed throughout the church. Besides using every space on church property, innumerable private homes have been used for study groups and workshops, mostly led by members of the congregation who volunteer to share their expertise. Much honor is due to the teachers, youth group advisors, discussion leaders, greeters, ushers, refreshment hosts, bulletin folders, newsletter stuffers, office equipment patrons, phone callers, stewardship visitors, neighborhood zone hosts, flower carriers, deliverers of the taperecorded services — all for spreading the Word as genuine "evangelists."

Diakonia

On Sunday, May 20, 1979, Charlotte Roads as moderator concluded her call to worship with this prayer: "We pray that our individual stewardship will become collectively sufficient to enable our church to reach its fullest potential of love and brotherhood in service not only within the confines of our church, but our town, our nation, and our world. Amen." Signs of consistent stretching toward Old North's fullest potential in service are evident in the extra efforts made beyond budgeted mission giving. Such projects have provided food, clothing, medical and agricultural supplies, and skilled guidance to people locally and around the world.

Two exercises in caring provided a direct strengthening of love and brotherhood in service: (1) the welcoming and settling of Kien, An, and Minh Tran from a Vietnamese refugee camp, the birth among us of their little girl, Hung Ngoc, and our continued efforts to bring their teenage daughter, An's mother, her sister, and her two children to our country; (2) the commitment of our congregation to the weekly feeding of a large group of "street people" at the Crombie Street Church in Salem which has resulted in a heightened awareness among us all of the pain of poverty and the preciousness of human dignity.

Koinonia

In February 1979 with a clear vision of the purpose of Christian fellowship, Rev. Francis Hood challenged the church to make real the words of the hymn: "Blest be the tie that binds our hearts in Christian love." Since then, every Sunday finds worshipers gathered for conversation over refreshments after services. Fellowship groups within the church

Christmas concert, 1983.

renewed their sense of belonging. A "neighborhood zone plan" was launched for strengthening the ties that bind and to make the church more responsive to household crises. Theme suppers, old-fashioned potlucks, Mother's Day breakfasts, the annual Christmas fair, two remarkably successful auctions, and a spring house tour all fanned the flame of fellowship within the parish. Active participation in the church's Essex South Association and the Massachusetts Conference work and a new Marblehead Interfaith Lay Council stretched the boundaries of belonging. The quarter-century fraternal tie with Temple Emanu-El was tightened with regular Thanksgiving eve services together and two pulpit exchanges per year. An ecumenical Ash Wednesday evensong and the annual summer singers' workshop bound together local church musicians. The gala Christmas concert each December drew upon the talents of Marblehead singers from every religious tradition in town, creating the demand for an open dress rehearsal to accommodate those who could not get a ticket for the evening performance, which sold out three years in a row.

Latreuo

On June 24, 1979, in honor of Marblehead's 350th birthday, the sanctuary overflowed as the parish gathered for a "Colonial Worship Service." With many dressed in authentic costumes, eighteenth-century music and prayers were heard along with a portion of one of Parson Barnard's sermons. Four of Old North's ministers (Gene Arnould, George Hooten, Francis Hood, and Ran Niehoff) and the senior deacon (Jim Clark) presided under "full wigs." The style of the service provided a bridge of understanding to link the town with its distant past; the participation of the four clergy provided a bridge of understanding to link the church with its recent past.

Meanwhile, on Sunday mornings it became customary for children to begin worship with their families, and after a few moments of dialogue designed especially for them, they were excused to their classes. Children's choirs soon began to lead worship on a regular basis, as the adult choir has been doing since 1925. Two outstanding operettas were written and conducted by Marie Stultz: *The Worthy Gift* at Christmas, 1980, and *The Tethered Colt* on Palm Sunday, 1982. Both productions featured young people from the church who showed fine talent. By the fall of 1983 over ninety-five members were singing for worship in one of the three choirs: Cecilia (ages six through eight), Parish Singers (age nine through high school), and the Adult Senior Choir. The added gifts of organist Richard Stultz's warm personality, quick wit, and accomplished musical expertise are immeasurable and have proved an invaluable asset to the life of Old North Church since August 1973. In November 1983 the fine Baroque-type harpsichord built by Dick as a memorial gift for Evelyn Hooten was freshly tuned and refinished, and the inner lid was enhanced with a nineteenth-century Marblehead vista by local artist and choir member Nancy Ferguson. It was dedicated as a symbol of the church's commitment to excellence in sacred music.

Noteworthy are the ongoing special services of worship: the dark mood and awe of the Tenebrae led by deacons and deaconesses following the annual Seder meal; the sparkle and magic of Christmas Eve candlelight services; the majesty and grandeur of Easter morning. A most joyfully weepy occasion occurred on January 25, 1981, when, surrounded by yellow ribbons tied on the church doors and pulpit, pinned to choir robes, coats, blouses, and blazers, a Service of Thanksgiving was held for the release of the American Embassy personnel held hostage in Iran. A white carnation tied with yellow ribbons was awarded along with a standing ovation to our faithful deacon Ralph Keller who had tolled the 1,800-pound church bell every day during their captivity as a symbol of our prayers for them.

Anytime the congregation gathers for worship it is an occasion of note.

Our Hebrew forebears bequeathed the concept of the Sabbath as a "sanc-tuary in time" — a divinely inspired challenge to pause regularly to count blessings, confess and be forgiven, pray for the needs of others, learn and reflect, and renew personal energies to live a life of love. The faithfulness of a church at worship is strengthened by how worshipers choose to treat each other. A note found in the collection plate one Sunday which had been penned by a visitor expresses it well: "The people we have met this morning are beautiful. We were warmly greeted at the door and seated. May all people know the love of God and the fellowship of man."

Epilogue:
Challenges and
Hopes for Our Future

THREE AND A HALF centuries of service and influence as a church in a relatively small community has proved to be a moving force in Marblehead that has extended beyond to include the Commonwealth and indeed, the nation. As a pebble dropped into a pool causes ripples of water to flow outward until they reach the farthest shore, so the Yankee influence of the First Church in Marblehead has spread far abroad.

A review of the past from early beginnings, through good times and bad, through periods of great thrust and energy and at times running at a slow trot, has found us to have arrived at this point in history. You have read with interest and pride the history of the First Church in Marblehead and the records show the events and persons as they have shaped the past into a rich heritage.

"We are surrounded by so great a cloud of witnesses ... let us run with perseverance the race that is set before us." (Hebrews 12:1) This is the challenge: that we become true to the past; the "cloud of witnesses" has given the present generation a foundation from which to work and a plan to "run the race that is before us." This is the challenge and the impetus, the force that causes us to look forward with hope.

The Old Town House, built in 1727, with the Old North tower in the background.

We do review the past in order that we might learn what has been good, what has been successful, what the influence of dedicated lives has meant, along with those things which have caused us grief and failure. History teaches us, for she is a good teacher, and we need to learn from her.

The church and the town are interwoven in their influence upon local lives. In no small way will the destiny of Marblehead be determined by the moral and spiritual power of First Church. In the past the church and the town were flowers of a single seed and children of the same parent. They grew and prospered together. Today, the church is delighted to function as part of an ecumenical team wherein all the religious congregations of Marblehead pool their resources to deal with community issues. There is no doubt that the future will demand the continued healthy exercise of such spiritual guidance.

It is evident that what lies ahead in the next fifty years for Old North Church and Marblehead, and certainly for the Judeo-Christian tradition and society-at-large, is the number of problems that must be addressed. The solutions may not be clear presently but the attempt to solve them is crucial. The following are issues that appear as we look into the future:

Technological Power and Human Identity

What lies ahead could in the next fifty years bring about a renaissance for the United States in terms of its prestige and power. American techological expertise (especially in the booming "high-tech" industries) promises great material reward and a certain yet unpredictable change in daily life-style and the way individuals perceive their worth. The mission and ministry of the church will remain as it has through the ages but will be challenged to struggle and cope with the technological revolution. The challenge of the biblical faith community is to spread its trust in God so as to breath sanity and articulate moral clarity in the midst of what could be a dehumanizing technological complexity. Churches and synagogues will have to play a larger role in community life. Greater importance will be placed upon the traditional values of family, friendship, and the mutual interdependence of countries. A symbol of the danger of greater reliance upon machinery is the way in which individual identity becomes a number in a computer bank. As technology grows and becomes more complex, Americans will become more intense in the search for religious meaning.

Ecumenical Leadership in a Changing Society

The boundaries which have separated Catholics, Protestants, and Jews will continue to be broken down; prejudice will be overcome by increased understanding, and self-centered ethnic loyalties will be replaced by a new sense of fellowship discovered while working side by side on societal issues. The results of increased intermarriage and a loosening of cultic rules and regulations will add to this interfaith activity; the Judeo-Christian community will present a more solid front to the secular society. How are expensive and innovative religious based programs to prosper? Only through a vital faith in the central ethics of the Judeo-Christian tradition will leadership be developed strong enough to cope with the dangers of bigotry in a world rapidly growing smaller.

Growth Among the Older Population

We are confronted by futurists whose predictions tell us that in coming decades there will be a more vigorous elderly population which will transform America (once youth oriented) into a mature society. Those who are sixty-five years of age and over will account for more than one out of every five persons in our country, and this ratio will alter the way Americans live and work. At present, our senior citizens represent an untapped resource and more efforts should be made to include their experience and their wisdom in community affairs. Religious organizations are well-positioned to incorporate elderly people into programs and projects designed to improve communal life. Congregations will become the social center and the spiritual resource to care for the individual needs of all generations — thanks to a more active contribution from retired people.

Young People in the Church

The future of the church and community lies in its storehouse of children. If Old North is to continue to be a power in the service of God and man it must view the presence of questioning and energetic youth not as a problem but as an opportunity. A renewed commitment to provide quality religious education must be made a priority. The next fifty years will see some changes as materials and methods are updated to include basic biblical background presented in a way that is relevant to our younger generations. The curriculum must engage an individual's attention in order to offer Christian moral direction that will help young people cope with the technical age. In addition, the education program should become more "clinical", offering youth in-person opportunities to meet and serve others in mission and outreach projects. As children become adolescents, the ministry to youth will need to be strengthened and supported by the whole congregation under the leadership of a staff person. To maintain a covenant relationship with young adults, Christian education should diversify its efforts to include programs for those men and women aged twenty to thirty-five and occasions where multigenerational learning and playing can occur.

Social Issues of the Larger Community

As a church we will be confronted by the challenge to address a growing number of societal needs that are not met by secular agencies and/or government funding. Recognizing that the heart of the Gospel is service through loving concern, the congregation will become more involved in supporting outreach programs to feed the hungry at our doorstep and around the world, to give aid and education to those who are powerless, and to provide church-sponsored low-income housing. The trend in the next five decades will be to involve individuals in helping work that is "hands on," where results are immediate and measurable. The example of Christian mission work which teaches self-help, thereby preserving dignity and freedom, should become the model for secular foreign aid efforts. Meanwhile, in Marblehead lay leaders will become actively involved in a pastoral ministry as partners with the clergy. A formal visitation program will emerge with staff supervision, especially tied to the maintenance of fellowship within neighborhood contexts. There will develop programs to provide transportation to and from congregational functions, more lay participation in calling on the sick and shut-in, increased presence of lay people in liturgy and teaching of special seminars.

Expansion Within the Workings of the Old North Church

Growing membership, increased activity, more pressing needs of the larger community all result in greater demands upon church leaders. There needs to be an increase in church staff, perhaps additional ordained clergy but certainly some carefully chosen key lay people with special skills and talents. An intriguing method of deploying effective leadership has been the recent practice of hiring part-time specialists for specific tasks from within the parish community rather than employing another full-time clergyman and assigning him/her a mixed job description. A likely vision of the church staff would include: senior minister, associate minister, director of religious education, minister/s of music, church administrator (or executive secretary), church office secretary/s, bookkeeper, secretary for parish life and fellowship, sexton/s, and housekeeper.

Growing pains have also put a strain on our limited facilities: larger assemblies at worship, more fellowship events, crowded Sunday School classes, bigger choirs, a doubling in the number of weddings and baptisms during the last four years, and the growth in church office activity have created an acute awareness of space and the best way to use it. If such trends continue it will be necessary to offer a third worship service and a second session of the Church School at the same time. The need for more room and more suitable use of what space is available includes such matters as parking space and barrier-free, accessible rest rooms. Careful attention to practical problems may even spark more creative ways to transport and gather people than we now foresee.

We who live today stand at the apex of a vast pyramid of human development, slowly accumulated through many years of struggle. We are heirs to all that has been accomplished to improve human life — all that has been dreamed and thought out, fought and died for, left behind for the guidance of future generations.

Today the church faces what is probably the greatest challenge history has ever known. Now, when millions of people are troubled, uncertain, threatened by nuclear holocaust, injustice, racism (and the list goes on), we have this rich deposit of inspiration and help left to us by the ancestors of our faith. Never has there been a time when the people of the church were more desperately in need of the comfort and courage of our faith tradition, its standards, and ideals by which to live, and above all, its abiding hope in the future. The contribution of the past cannot be underestimated for it has given us perspective on our situations and inspiration for our task to make life abundant as the future moves toward us.

If we are true to what has been given us, remembering — and thus embodying — the heritage of our church, we can go forward into the future unafraid. Looking into the future can be a risky business unless the challenge and the hopes are empowered by a deep, abiding faith in the ways of God, our source of life and purpose, and our Fellow-Traveler through history.

Gerald K. O'Neill of Princeton University stated: "Unless we do something violently stupid with our future, the eternals of hope and love and laughter will still be there."

Page from Parson John Barnard's book of sermon discourses.

Appendices

Our Heritage Silver

The antique sacramental silver owned by the Old North Church is a priceless heritage, donated by early members in devotion to their church and in memory of loved ones. It is considered by experts to be among the rarest and most valuable church silver in the United States, and some of the pieces dating from the seventeenth and eighteenth centuries have been recorded in authoritative books on early American silver. The set consists of a baptismal bowl, four flagons, two plates, twelve cups or beakers, and a spoon, all of solid silver, and four baskets which are Sheffield plate.

In 1953, during the pastorate of the Reverend Robert S. Balfe, the church committee authorized the printing of a booklet concerning the heritage silver entitled *The Communion Silver, Its Makers and Its Donors*. It was written by Zulette Potter, devoted church member and local historian. The story and description of each piece may be found in this booklet, which is still available in the church office.

In January 1908 the church voted to adopt individual communion cups for the use of the congregation, and these were first used on May 3, 1908. The ministers and deacons continued using the heritage cups and flagons which were set out on the communion table, while the small glass cups were served to worshipers in their pews, a custom continued today.

In 1931, during the pastorate of the Reverend Dwight L. Cart, Yale University made an offer to purchase the entire silver collection for $25,000, or three particular pieces for $10,000. The congregation unanimously rejected the offer, some considering it sacrilege even to consider the idea. Some ten years earlier an equally unsuccessful attempt had been made by wealthy patrons of the Boston Museum of Fine Arts to purchase some or all the silver to add to the museum's collection of rare church silver.

On Sunday morning, June 8, 1969, the congregation was shocked to hear the Reverend George Hooten announce from the pulpit that the entire collection had been stolen from the large safe in the basement of the church. William Giles, senior deacon at the time, discovered the wrecked and empty safe when he went to get the baptismal bowl for use during the service. Evidence indicated that the thieves had forced French doors used as an emergency exit from the sanctuary — their abandoned tools were found on the ground outside these doors. They made their way to the basement and, using sledgehammer and crowbar, smashed the big safe open. With no one around the church premises from Friday noon till Sunday morning, they could work at their leisure and with light, since the basement walls are made of stone, are thick and soundproof, and have no windows.

For many years the silver had been kept in a bank vault, but when the church was given a large fireproof safe the trustees decided to install it in the basement and to store the silver there for more convenient access. Few parishioners knew of this arrangement, and only the senior deacon and deaconess had the combination to the safe's lock. No one will ever know how the thieves knew where to look.

Because of the historic value of the silver, estimated between $250,000 and $400,000, the theft received nationwide attention from the news media. Local police, believing that it was a professional rather than a local job, enlisted the aid of the FBI. But it was not until early in 1970 that the first telephone contact was made with Dr. Hooten, offering to return the silver for a ransom. Everyone was relieved that it had not been melted down or spirited out of the country!

After numerous phone calls and negotiations with intermediaries, the silver was brought to Dr. Hooten at the parsonage during March 1970. The trustees had authorized the payment of a $15,000 ransom which was to be paid in cash, $5,000 each time a portion of the silver was returned, in three installments. Dr. Hooten examined the silver carefully, and after the final delivery he determined that one piece was missing, an especially valuable beaker. He coolly refused to turn over the entire $5,000, and the intermediary finally left with only $4,000.

Some months later a brown-paper-wrapped package arrived by mail at the church office. There was no return address; the postmark was smudged; and the address was formed from cutout printed letters pasted on. The church secretary immediately thought of the missing beaker, since the package was about the right size. When she opened it, there was the beaker, neatly wrapped in tissue paper, but with the inscription and the foliate scroll decoration completely burnished off. The maker's stamp of Hull and Sanderson on the bottom of the base was still there, identifying the cup beyond a doubt.

The violated beaker was taken to J. Herbert Gebelein, Boston silversmith, for restoration. It was determined that the buffed areas were too thin to be reengraved, but Gebelein's engraver, Harold A. Small, was able to reproduce the original foliate scrolls and the inscription by placing the reproduction in alternate areas on the sides of the cup. Fortunately, this cup was one of the pieces pictured in a book on early American silver, so the engraver had a reference to work from.

The publicity attending the theft of the silver and its ransom caused the church to take a hard look at the responsibility of owning inherited assets valued at more than $250,000. Some newer members advocated selling the silver and "giving the money to the poor," claiming that it was unchristian to keep it when there was so much need in the world. A committee was appointed to study the options, including sale in whole or in part, donating or loaning to a museum, methods of storage if kept, insurance, and the legal aspects of selling legacies left as memorials.

This committee's comprehensive report was received by the 1971 annual meeting. No immediate action was taken, but the meeting voted to call for a written ballot by mail to enable all members of the church to participate in the ultimate decision. This was done, and of 336 members returning ballots only 26 favored selling the heritage silver.

Today our beautiful old silver is used on special occasions, and the church committee is responsible for its safekeeping in a bank vault. Regular use is made of new memorial silver donated after the theft and before the recovery of the antique pieces.

Under the Golden Cod

First Members of the Newly Organized Congregational Church as of August 13, 1684

Samuel Cheever*

Ruth Cheever

Moses Maverick*

Eunice Maverick*

Ambrose Gale*

Richard Reith*

William Bartoll*

Mary Bartoll*

George Bondfield*

William Beal

Benjamin Parmiter*

Edward Read*

Francis Girdler*

John Merritt*

Mary Merritt*

Samuel Sandin*

Charity Sandin*

Benjamin Gale*

Deliverance Gale*

John Stacey*

Agnes Stacey*

John Seaward*

Sarah Ward

Jane Pitman*

Elizabeth Conant*

Mary Dixey*

Mary Merritt*

Elizabeth Legg*

Miriam Pederick*

Elizabeth Watts*

Anna Symmes*

Abigail Clarke*

Sarah Henly*

Sarah Buckly

Margaret Ellis*

Joanna Hawley*

Dorcas Pedrick*

Sarah Dodd*

Mary Fortune*

Elizabeth Russell*

Mary Ferguson*

Miriam Hanniford*

Abigail Merret*

Mary Rolls*

Abigail Hinds*

Charity Pitman*

Mary Clattery*

Jane Blackler*

Rebecca Carder*

Grace Coos*

Mary Doliber*

Alice Darby*

Elizabeth Gatchell*

Elizabeth Glass*

* Denotes signers of the May 24, 1684, petition requesting separation from the Salem Church.

Old North Church Ministers

The Rev. John Avery	1635-
Mr. William Walton	1638-1668
The Rev. Samuel Cheever	1668-1724
The Rev. John Barnard	1716-1770
The Rev. William Whitwell	1762-1781
The Rev. Ebenezer Hubbard	1783-1800
The Rev. Samuel Dana	1801-1837
The Rev. Samuel Cozzens	1832-1837
The Rev. Mark A. H. Niles	1837-1844
The Rev. Edward A. Lawrence	1845-1854
The Rev. Benjamin Allen	1854-1872
The Rev. John H. Williams	1873-1883
The Rev. S. Linton Bell	1884-1902
The Rev. Nicholas Van der Pyl, D.D.	1903-1907
The Rev. John W. Barnett, Ph.D.	1907-1910
The Rev. Leslie C. Greeley	1910-1924
The Rev. Harris G. Hale, D.D.	1925-1930
The Rev. Dwight L. Cart, D.D.	1930-1936
The Rev. Oliver F. Wiese	1937-1941
The Rev. Thomas A. Goodwin, D.D.	1942-1949
The Rev. Robert S. Balfe	1950-1956
The Rev. Eric M. Rickard, Jr.	1956-1960
The Rev. Kendall Link (Assistant)	1958-1961
The Rev. George M. Hooten, Jr., D.D.	1961-1978
The Rev. Ralph E. Short (Assistant)	1962-1965
The Rev. Charles F. Hood (Associate)	1965-
The Rev. Eugene R. Arnould (Assistant)	1971-1975
The Rev. Howard H. MacMullen, Jr. (Assistant)	1975-1978
The Rev. Randall H. Niehoff, D. Min.	1979-

Chronology

1635   Church gathered, worship services in homes

1648   Meetinghouse built on Old Burial Hill

1684   Organized as Congregational Church on August 13

1695   Church on Franklin Street built

1716   Second Congregational Church formed

1717   First Association of Clergy in Essex County

1762   Present pulpit bible received

1773   Paul Revere baptismal bowl given by Dr. Lemmon

1817   Sunday school commenced in chapel on Pearl Street on May 18

1824   Present church built

1827   Essex South Association of Congregational Churches formed in the sanctuary of Old North Church on May 8

1858   Third Church (South) formed

1869   Parsonage on High Street built

1877   Third (South) Church destroyed by fire and congregation returned to Old North

1879   Parish House built next to church

1886   Rebuilt front of church, removed pulpit and box pews, and replaced Paul Revere bell with the present bell. Revere bell was originally installed in Franklin Street Church in 1818 and is now in Pleasant Hill, Tennessee.

1923   New organ installed

1935   Restored old pulpit

1943   Incorporated - adopted by-laws

1950   Rebuilt parish house

1964   United with United Church of Christ

1971   New organ installed in balcony - narthex remodeled

1981   Parsonage at 23 High Street sold

Illustrations and Credits

The illustrations in *Under The Golden Cod* came from varied sources and the Book Committee and the publisher are deeply grateful to all who so generously loaned existing material and provided new photographs for consideration and possible inclusion. Special thanks are due Bowden Osborne for making available to us his magnificent collection of historic photographs and memorabilia of Marblehead and for his patience in helping fulfill our requirements.

The publisher would also like to acknowledge the unstinting help and advice of M. Swift & Sons of Hartford, Connecticut, in the process of gold embossing with Glitterfoil® the representation of Old North's codfish weathervane on the front cover of this volume. Not only did they lend us their own die, made some years previously for their *Portfolio of Early American Weathervanes*, but their staff provided invaluable technical help in achieving a successful result.

In the following, all illustrations are listed chronologically as they appear in the book. The abbreviated title of each is followed, where known, by the photographer's or delineator's name, the source, and the page number on which the illustration appears.

Jacket photo and photo on which endleaf design is based by John Ferguson.

Foreword from Parson John Barnard's book of sermon-discourses / Howard Bantley photo, x

Old North sign / John Ferguson photo, 6

Old Burial Hill marker / John Ferguson photo, 9

First Meeting House plaque / Howard Bantley photo, 11

Original pew / John Ferguson photo, 13

Foot warmer / John Ferguson photo, 19

Sketch of First Meeting House / Bicentennial booklet published 1884, 20

Old Burial Hill graveyard / John Ferguson photo, 22

Parson Barnard House / Photo attributed to Samuel Chamberlain / Bowden Osborne collection, 26

Parson Barnard bible / Robert Gotschall photo, 28

Early fish flake or fence / Bowden Osborne collection, 31

Gravestone of John Barnard / Howard Bantley photo, 33

Sketch of Franklin Street Meeting House / Bicentennial booklet published 1884, 39

The *Hannah* / Painting by unknown artist / Bowden Osborne collection, 41

Gravestone of William Whitwell / Howard Bantley photo, 43

Old North in 1860 / Church archives, 46

Snow *America* / Watercolor by M. Corne / Bowden Osborne collection, 48

Ship *Mary* / Painting by Wm. York / Bowden Osborne collection, 49

William Reed / Painting by unknown artist / John Ferguson photo, 53

Old North in the mid-1800s / Church archives, 56

Lyon's shoe shop / Bowden Osborne collection, 58

1854 Church records / John Ferguson photo, 59

Third Congregational (South) Church / Bowden Osborne collection, 60

Parsonage at 23 High Street / Church archives, 63

200th anniversary, 1884 / Church archives, 68

Great fire of 1888 / Bowden Osborne collection, 69

Old North in 1890 / Bowden Osborne collection, 70

The *Alice* leaves harbor, 1891 / Bowden Osborne collection, 71

View from Crocker Park, 1898 / Bowden Osborne collection, 72

Old North interior, early 1900s / Church archives, 73

View from Abbot Hall, circa 1915 / Bowden Osborne collection, 78

Lobster Shanty / Bowden Osborne collection, 80

Old North interior, late 1920s / Courtesy Mrs. Wilson H. Roads, 84

Five ministers at the 300th anniversary

Indexes

NAME INDEX

OLD NORTH CHURCH INDEX

TOWN OF MARBLEHEAD INDEX

GENERAL INDEX

In Appreciation

The Book Committee greatly appreciates the generosity of the sponsors listed below whose financial support helped make publication of this book possible.

Lorraine and Merrilee Albright
Lydia F. Ayer
Barnard Club, in memory of departed members
Mrs. S. Whitney Bradley
The Kenneth Buchanan Family
Mary E. Cady
In memory of Elizabeth S. Campbell
Frederick W. and Cynthia N. Carone
The Chadwick Family
Mr. and Mrs. Stanley J. Evans
Stephen H. Fagg
In memory of Edward W. Farrell
Mr. and Mrs. John H. Ferguson
In memory of Mr. and Mrs. Thomas E. Ferguson
Dorothy C. Gorman
Robert and Day Gotschall
Mrs. Samuel McK. Gray
In memory of Laura T. Griswold
In memory of Garrison Kent Hall
Mr. and Mrs. Clarence L. Hamm
Georgianna Henderson
Mr. and Mrs. Richard D. Hill
In memory of Caroline M. Hills
Mr. and Mrs. Frederick E. Hood
Katherine Howes, in memory of William Howes
In memory of Dorothy R. Hunt
Marian R. Irving

In memory of Mildred Hammond Joyce
Mrs. Charles H. Learoyd
Kim Perry Leonsis and Theodore J. Leonsis
Norma MacMullen Lord
Mr. and Mrs. Philip H. Lord
In memory of Harvey Lamond Macaulay
In honor of Dr. and Mrs. George R. Miller, Jr.
Evelyn M. Ohm
William W. Peabody
Madeline Peach, in memory of her mother, Lena Power
In memory of Robert P. Perkins
Dr. and Mrs. Willard Perry, Jr.
Mr. and Mrs. Arthur P. Poor
In memory of Samuel Roads
Mr. and Mrs. Richard S. Robie, Jr.
Mr. and Mrs. Albert C. Rogers
In memory of Ruth A. Rundle
The John E. Searle Family
Mr. and Mrs. Philip H. Seaver
In memory of Paul Simpson
In memory of Edith B. and Marquis S. Smith
Robert, Helen, Ava, and Christian Steenstrup
Edythe M. Storrow
Mr. and Mrs. Howard H. Ward
In memory of Marjorie B. Webber
David K. Young